REVISE YOUR 'S' GRADE HISTORY

Revised Edition

by

Charles Rigg
Jerry Teale
Chris Mackay

© *Messrs. Rigg, Teale, Mackay, 2000*
ISBN 0 7169 3231 8

The Scottish Certificate of Education Examination Questions
are reprinted by special permission of
THE SCOTTISH QUALIFICATIONS AUTHORITY

ROBERT GIBSON · Publisher
17 Fitzroy Place, Glasgow, G3 7SF.

INTRODUCTION

This book is intended to be used by candidates sitting the Standard Grade examination in the year 2000 and beyond. It is based on the Standard Grade History arrangements published in 1998.

Candidates will find it useful as a study aid for revision, for self-testing and for highlighting parts of the syllabus where further study is required.

The book covers the five most popular topics, namely:

(i)   Unit 1, Context B — Changing Life in Scotland and Britain: 1830s–1930s.

(ii)   Unit 1, Context C — Changing Life in Scotland and Britain: 1880s–Present Day.

(iii)   Unit 2, Context B — International Cooperation and Conflict: 1890s–1920s.

(iv)   Unit 3, Context C — People and Power: Russia 1914–1941.

(v)   Unit 3, Context D — People and Power: Germany 1918–1939.

CONTENTS

UNIT 1 — Changing Life in Scotland and Britain
Context B: 1830s–1930s

UNIT 1 — Changing Life in Scotland and Britain
Context C: 1880s to Present Day

UNIT 2 — International Cooperation and Conflict
Context B: 1890s–1920s
Part 1 — 1890–1914

Part 2 — 1914–1918

Part 3 — 1918–1928

UNIT 3 — People and Power
Context C: Russia 1914–1941

Part 1 — 1914–1917

Part 2 — 1917–1924

Part 3 — 1924–1941

UNIT 3 — People and Power
       Context D: Germany 1918–1939

UNIT 1 — Changing Life in Scotland and Britain

CONTEXT B: 1830s–1930s

1

Population Growth and Distribution

Population Growth

	Scotland	Britain
1831	2·36 million	16·3 million
1851	2·88 million	21 million
1901	4·47 million	37 million
1931	4·84 million	45 million

Reasons for Population Growth 1831–1939

After the Registration Act of 1836 there is clear evidence to show the effect of *birth rates* and *death rates* on the growth of population.

Year	Birth Rate	Death Rate	Comment
1838 1871	30·3 35·0	22·4 22·6	During this period the rising birth rate contributed to the growth of population at a time when the death rate remained reasonably stable.
1881 1911 1938	33·9 24·3 15·1	18·9 14·6 11·6	During this period there was a big fall in both the birth rate and the death rate. The rate of population growth slowed down.

(a) *Reasons for rise in birth rate 1831–1871*

    Early marriages — Children, from an early age, could bring money into the family.

(b) *Reasons for a decline in the birth rate 1871–1939*

    (i) *Children could no longer work* and bring in money following the 1870 Education Act (England) and 1872 Education Act (Scotland).

(ii) *The middle classes wanted better living standards* so they had smaller families.

(iii) *Knowledge of birth control* became better known in the 20th century with the setting-up of Marie Stopes clinics.

(iv) *During World War One, British losses totalled 0·75 million* men and there was also many more left wounded. The absence of so many young men after the war contributed to the drop in the birth rate.

(c) *Reasons for a fall in the death rate after 1871*

(i) *Improvements in town conditions* brought about by a better water supply, sewerage and housing. As a result, cholera was wiped out.

(ii) *Better and cheaper food* supply brought about by improved railway system and cheap imports of food from abroad.

(iii) *Improved medical knowledge* — Lister's work on *antiseptics* and Simpson's work on *anaesthetics* made operations a lot more successful.

(iv) *Better welfare provision* — The Liberal Government, 1906–1914, introduced measures to care for children (Provision of School Meals Act, 1906), unemployed (National Insurance Act, 1911) and the aged (Old Age Pensions, 1909).

In 1880 a person would be expected to live to the age of 43, by 1939 a person would be expected to live to the age of 65 years.

Redistribution in Countryside and in Towns

Growth of towns

	1841	1881	1931
Aberdeen	64 778	105 000	170 000
Dundee	60 553	140 000	176 000
Edinburgh	138 182	295 000	439 000
Glasgow	274 533	587 000	1 088 000

In 1831, less than one person in every three stayed in a town of 5000 people or more. By 1881, almost half the population, one person in every two, stayed in a town of 5000 people or more. By 1939, almost two out of every three people stayed in a town of 5000 people or more.

The growth of towns was a result of

(i) *growth in population;*

(ii) *migration* of people from the countryside to the towns in search of employment;

(iii) *arrival of Irish immigrants* in search of employment.

The Effects of the Growth of Population and Urbanisation

1. *Farms* had to increase production to feed a growing population.

2. *Transport* had to improve to allow food to reach the towns faster. The growth of railways provided the means of doing this.

3. *Industry* had to expand to create employment and more manufactured goods.

4. *Social problems* were created as towns became overcrowded.

2

Highland Migration within Britain and Overseas

The Highland Problem in the mid-19th Century

(i) The land was *over-populated* to make farming profitable — in 1830, 50% of the Scottish population lived in the Highlands.

(ii) The climate and poor quality of soil made *arable farming unproductive.*

(iii) Landowners saw an opportunity to get a higher rent from introducing *sheep*. However, few people were needed to look after sheep.

(iv) In the 1840s, the *potato blight* created a serious shortage of food.

The Highland Clearances

There had been clearances in the Highlands before the 1840s, most notably in Sutherland, but it was not until the 1840s that the Highlanders left in large numbers.

The case for the landowner

1. The landowner could become richer if he introduced *sheep*, which required little in the way of looking after yet produced good profits.

2. Many tenants were unable to pay their rent so that the landowner himself was in danger of getting into *debt*, for example, Lord MacDonald of Skye.

3. A *long-term solution* had to be found to the Highland problem and emigration was an attractive solution. Landowners could not give handouts of money or oats indefinitely.

4. The landowner paid substantial sums of money to *pay the fare* and food for the overseas crossing.

The case against the landowner

1. Landowners put *profit* before human consideration.

2. *Evictions* were carried out by the factor without consideration for the elderly in particular. Houses were burned down as soon as the tenants left, so that they could not return.

3. The *journey* was long and difficult.

4. If the landowner had spent the same *money* on his own estate as he did on paying his tenants' passage abroad, there might have been no need for so many to emigrate.

As a result of the Highland Clearances, many communities in the Highlands were broken up. Without work, many of the young and most energetic left for jobs in the industrial areas of Britain such as Glasgow. The textile mills at New Lanark had Highlanders who had left their homes in search of employment. Others decided to emigrate overseas.

Emigration from the Highlands

The extreme hardship of life in the Highlands persuaded many to look overseas for new opportunities and a fresh start in life. These people were *pulled* by the promise of:

   (i) employment

   (ii) good wages and prosperity

   (iii) health through living in a good climate

   (iv) plenty of land.

Others were *pushed* by Highland landowners who wished to 'clear' their land of impoverished tenants and reluctantly made a long, demanding journey to an unknown country.

In the 20th century emigration continued with many heading for America or Canada. However, when America was hit by massive unemployment in the 1930s, the numbers leaving for the USA dropped dramatically.

The Effect of Highland Migration on the Highlands

The result of the movement of population away from the Highlands had a devastating effect on that part of Scotland by the end of the 19th century:

   (i) The clans were broken up with the clearances.
  (ii) Clan chiefs became landowners looking for a profit.
 (iii) Gaelic was spoken less.
 (iv) The population was made up of older people.
  (v) Many communities were completely destroyed by the clearances.
 (vi) The Crofters Act of 1886 allowed the old way of life to be enjoyed by some.

3

Irish Immigration to Scotland

Throughout the 19th century, the Irish arrived in Scotland in search of jobs, food and shelter. As the figures below illustrate, the level of Irish immigration was particularly high in the 1840s during the potato famine in Ireland.

Irish — born in Scotland (population census)
1841 — 126 321 (4·8% of total population)
1851 — 207 307 (7·2% of total population)
1881 — 218 745 (5·9% of total population)
1931 — 124 296 (2·6% of total population)

The arrival of the Irish contributed significantly to the growth of towns like Glasgow and Dundee in particular.

Parts of Scotland where the Irish settled

Cities

(a) Glasgow — by 1851, 18·2% of the population was Irish born.

(b) Dundee — by 1850, 19% of the population was of Irish origin.

(c) Edinburgh and Leith — in 1851, about 6% of the city.

Counties

(d) Ayrshire and the South-West; Dumbarton, Renfrew and Lanark.

The impact of the arrival of the Irish was far greater in Scotland than in England because of the concentration of the Irish in the areas of Glasgow and Dundee and the fact that England was a larger host country. In 1861, for example, only 3% of England's population was Irish born, whereas in Scotland it was more than twice that at 6·7%

What Impact did the Irish Immigrants Make on the Scottish Community?

Employment

(i) Largely *unskilled* work, e.g. labourers on roads, canals, railways, weaving, coal mining.

(ii) *Seasonal work* in agriculture, e.g. harvesting.

(iii) Irish *females* worked in textile factories or domestic service.

(iv) Irish were prepared to take jobs at a *lower wage* than the native Scottish population and this caused resentment amongst the native population.

Religion

(i) Most of the Irish who emigrated in the 1840s were Catholics.

(ii) Conflict between the native Protestant population and the Irish Catholic population led to the holding of Orange Order marches where physical violence occurred.

(iii) In the 1870s and 1880s, many Protestant Irish arrived from Ulster (Northern Ireland) and this served to increase, particularly in Glasgow, the Catholic/Protestant divide.

Sport

The Irish community stuck together and formed their own football teams such as Edinburgh Hibernian (1875) and Glasgow Celtic Football Club

(1887), which still exist today, and Dundee Hibernian, which changed its name to Dundee United in the 20th century.

Social

Many of those who arrived were poor, badly clothed and poorly educated. They were not warmly welcomed and tended to live together in Irish communities. Their arrival in such large numbers in concentrated areas gave rise to social problems.

(i) *Housing* — There was a shortage of housing and many stayed in over-crowded hovels.

(ii) *Poor Rates* — Parishes viewed the arrival of the Irish as a likely burden on the poor rates in the 1830s, and tried to pressurise the Irish to move on.

(iii) *Poverty* — Some resorted to begging and thieving to survive, and solace (comfort) was sought in drink.

(iv) *Education* — After 1872, many Catholic Irish stayed out of schools run by School Boards, since the Boards would not guarantee the religious character of their schools.

4

Technological Change and its Effect on Developments in Railways

Background

(i) The first railway to be built was opened up in 1825 between Stockton and Darlington. As a result of the success of that railway and the Liverpool/Manchester railway (1830) there followed, in the 1830s and 1840s, a period of *railway mania*, during which a network of railways sprang up throughout Britain.

(ii) In the 1830s, the Government followed a policy of *laissez-faire* and did not want to interfere in the running of the railways. Due to the large number of accidents to both passengers and railway workers, the Government had to change its policy and pass laws to control railways.

(iii) Building of railways was hard work since there was very little technology. *Irish navvies* carried out the work using picks, shovels and wheel-barrows. Crude dynamite was used for blasting through rock, and there were many deaths and injuries in the construction of railways.

(iv) Not everyone welcomed railways.

   (a) *Landowners and farmers* feared that the countryside would be destroyed and that farm animals would be affected so that, for example, hens would stop laying eggs. There was also a worry that sparks from the engine would set fire to the thatched-roof houses.

   (b) Owners of *canals*, *coach companies* and *turnpikes* saw the railways as a threat to their existence.

(v) Railways were expensive to build and money was raised through the issue of *shares*. People bought shares because they thought they would make money. One person, George Hudson, became known as the 'railway king' as he bought shares in many companies in the thirties and forties. He eventually became bankrupt due to financial irregularities.

Government Policy

Although an Act of Parliament had to be passed before a railway could be built, the Government, at first, stuck to a policy of non-intervention. However, it had to change its policy in the interests of public safety.

1844 Railway Act — Each railway company had to run at least one train in each direction every day with *third class* covered carriages. They had to stop at every station and charge a low fare which was not to be higher than *1 penny a mile*.

1846 Railway Gauge Act — All railway lines had to use a railway gauge (distance between the rails) of 4 ft 8½ inches. Some lines had used a broader gauge of 7 ft before this.

1889 Regulation of Railways Act — Following the deaths of 80 people and injury to over 250 others, in June 1889, in a railway accident in Ireland, the Government acted quickly to make railways safer by making continuous brakes and block signalling compulsory.

During World War One — During the war the Government took control of the many railway companies and nationalised them.

Railways Act 1921 — The Government did not wish to keep the railways nationalised after the war. Instead

(i) *Four large companies*, the Southern, the Great Western, the London Midland and Scottish and the London and North Eastern Railways were formed out of the 120 companies which existed in 1920.

(ii) A *National Wages Board* was set up to settle wages and conditions.

Advances in Technology

Process	Position in 1830	Improvements
Building of railways	Largely by pick and shovel, horses and gunpowder.	Steam-powered machinery to get through rock.
Building bridges	Many magnificent bridges were built at this time as a result of brilliant engineers like Brunel.	Technology to build bridges over the Tay (1876) and the Forth (1890) although the Tay collapsed in 1879 and had to be rebuilt. These bridges opened up railway transport in the east of Scotland.
Locomotives	(i) Stephenson's *Rocket* in 1829 had a 6ft boiler and was able to reach 29 m.p.h.	As boilers became larger the speed of the train increased. The average speed in 1830 of a train was 15 m.p.h. By 1845, the average speed was up to 37 m.p.h. By the 1930s, average speeds were well over 50 m.p.h. and a world record of 126 m.p.h. had been achieved in 1938 by the *Mallard*.
	(ii) Locomotives were steam driven	Steam still dominated but a *diesel* service started in Blackpool (1928) and an *electric* passenger service from London to Brighton (1933).

Process	Position in 1830	Improvements
Signals	Hand signals	(i) Mechanically operated signals replaced hand operated signals after 1841.
		(ii) Electrically operated signals appeared in the early 20th century.
		(iii) By 1845, the new telegraph system was in use in most lines.
Braking	Trains sometimes had to make emergency stops by going into reverse. There were no brakes on individual carriages.	In 1889 all carriages had to have brakes.
Passenger comfort	Railway wagons were built to transport goods like coal. Passenger transport was very much a secondary consideration.	(i) Third class carriages were given seats and a roof.
		(ii) First and second class carriages became more luxurious with upholstered seating.
		(iii) Sleeping cars (1873), restaurant cars (1879), steam-heated carriages (1884) and lavatories in corridor trains (1892) were introduced by some of the bigger companies.

Impact of railways on industry — The railways boosted the economy in the middle of the 19th century and stimulated the coal and iron industries in particular. Employment opportunities, cheaper prices and higher profits created prosperity. The diagram below illustrates how industry in Scotland changed as a result of advances in railway technology through the 1830s–1930s period.

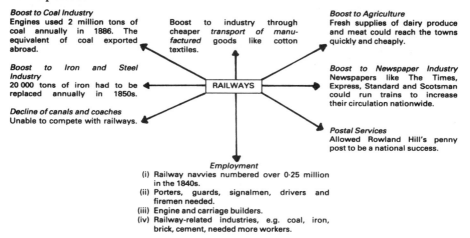

Boost to Coal Industry
Engines used 2 million tons of coal annually in 1886. The equivalent of coal exported abroad.

Boost to Iron and Steel Industry
20 000 tons of iron had to be replaced annually in 1850s.

Decline of canals and coaches
Unable to compete with railways.

Boost to industry through cheaper *transport of manufactured* goods like cotton textiles.

RAILWAYS

Boost to Agriculture
Fresh supplies of dairy produce and meat could reach the towns quickly and cheaply.

Boost to Newspaper Industry
Newspapers like The Times, Express, Standard and Scotsman could run trains to increase their circulation nationwide.

Postal Services
Allowed Rowland Hill's penny post to be a national success.

Employment
(i) Railway navvies numbered over 0·25 million in the 1840s.
(ii) Porters, guards, signalmen, drivers and firemen needed.
(iii) Engine and carriage builders.
(iv) Railway-related industries, e.g. coal, iron, brick, cement, needed more workers.

5

Technological Change and its Effect on Developments in Coal Mining

The Importance of Coal to the Economy, 1830–1913

In the 19th century coal was king. Demand came from a variety of sources as the diagram below illustrates.

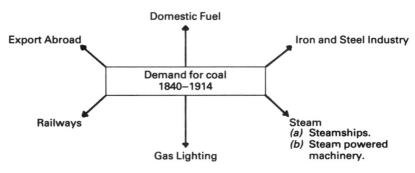

Domestic Fuel

Export Abroad

Iron and Steel Industry

Demand for coal
1840–1914

Railways

Steam
(a) Steamships.
(b) Steam powered machinery.

Gas Lighting

Importance of Coal to the Economy, 1918–1939

After World War One, the British coal industry went into decline because:

1. Other countries like Germany, Poland and America produced cheaper coal. As a result, Britain's *coal exports fell*.

2. *Domestic demand fell* due to the appearance of alternative fuels such as electricity, oil and gas.

3. Many British *mines were old* and exhausted. As a result they had become unproductive.

4. In comparison to other countries, there had been a *failure to invest in machinery*.

Growth of Coal Production

Year	Output (million tons)	Exports
1830	16	
1850	49·4	6·8%
1900	225·2	25·9%
1913	287	33·3%
1933	208	20·0%

The substantial growth in coal output, as illustrated in the table above, owed much to the technological advances which took place in mining during the period.

Advances in Mining Technology

Process	1830	Technological Advances
Ventilation	Fire buckets to draw fresh air through the pit.	Ventilation fans were introduced in 1860.
Lighting	Davy safety lamp replaced candles.	Electric lighting was introduced in 1880s.
Lowering workers down the mine shaft	Horse-gin	Steam or electrical power was used to raise cages up and down the shaft at the end of the 19th century.

Process	1830	Technological Advances
Haulage	Female labour climbing almost vertical ladders.	Iron cages were used to raise full tubs of coal. Pit ponies were used to pull wagons down the pit.
Blasting	Gunpowder with a fuse.	Gelignite with a detonator was introduced in the 1870s.
Flooding	Watt's steam engine.	More powerful engines,
Roof supports	Wooden pit props or pillars of coal.	Replaced by metal props which would not rot and collapse.
Cutting the coal	Pick, mell and wedge.	In Scotland, a coal cutting machine was first used in Coatbridge in 1864. Coal cutting machinery was slow to be adopted.

1. In comparison to abroad, the small British pits were slow to mechanise in the 20th century. In 1900, only 1·5% of British coal was cut by machinery compared to 25% in America.

2. In Scotland, coal cutting machinery was adopted more quickly than in England. By 1920, 34% of Scottish coal was machine-cut and within eight years had risen to 60%.

3. Mine owners were reluctant to invest in new machinery between the wars because of the possibility of nationalisation. In particular, countries like Germany had introduced conveyor systems to speed up the haulage of coal.

N.B. Technology played its part in the expansion of the industry but it was the failure to more fully modernise in the 20th century that resulted in other countries, such as Germany and America, taking Britain's overseas market.

Changes in Employment and in Working Conditions in the Mines

1. **Workforce** before 1842 was made up of:

   (a) *Children* — The youngest who acted as *trappers*, opening and closing doors. These children could be as young as four years old and work a 12-hour day in dark, damp conditions.

   (b) *Women* — Older children, about 11 years of age, and women would act as *bearers*, carrying heavy loads of coal to the surface. They would work 12 hours a day for six days a week.

   (c) *Men* — Worked as *hewers* cutting the coal. They paid the bearers for taking the coal to the surface. The hewer was then paid by the coal manager.

   Following the 1842 Mines Act, *children* under the age of ten and all *females* were forbidden to work underground in mines. Women continued to work at the surface of the mine.

2. **Nature of the work**

   (a) Coal mining was very *dangerous*. Despite improvements in technology, there were many deaths and injuries sustained in the coal pits. There were various reasons for the high casualty rate as the examples below illustrate:

Year	Location	Accident and Cause	Number of deaths
1877	High Blantyre	Gas explosion caused by a naked lamp as two brothers laid rails.	1
1877	High Blantyre	Gas explosion caused by a naked lamp.	200
1882	Silverdale (Ayrshire)	Gas explosion caused by a miner using his safety lamp to light his pipe.	2
1894	Montgomery	The winding steel rope broke and the miners in the cage were hurled to their death at the pit bottom.	4
1908	Kilmarnock	Men using gelignite to carry out blasting were killed either because the shot went off prematurely or there was a delay in the shot taking effect so the men went to investigate.	4
1909	Caprington (Ayrshire)	An old working place, 300 yards from the main shaft, subsided with the result that water from the River Irvine flooded the pit	10
1927	Galston	100 tons of boulder clay, sand and gravel tumbled down without warning. One victim was not found, the other died from suffocation.	2

(b) There was little in the way of *protective clothing* and it was not until the 1930s that a helmet made from compressed paper replaced the cloth cap.

(c) Conditions were *unhealthy* and those involved in the cutting of the coal at the coal face suffered from lung diseases which in later life made breathing very difficult. Coal dust got into cuts and left the miners with black sores.

(d) It was very *hot* down the mine and each miner took with him plenty of tea or water to replace the sweat that was lost. The miner's food was carried in a tin so that the *rats* would not get to it.

(e) *Pit ponies* were valued since they carried out a lot of the haulage in the pits. A pony's refusal to enter a mine road was taken as a warning of a likely roof fall.

3. Wages and accommodation

(a) In 1830, wages were quite good in comparison to agricultural work and unskilled factory work. The *hewer* paid the bearer and this encouraged hewers to marry early and have a family. His wife and children would then help him in his work.

(b) Reasonable *houses* were provided although they varied in quality. This was provided by the owners at a very low rent.

(c) Wages amounted to about 70% of the mine owners' costs. If the price of coal went down, as it did in the 20th century, then the mine owners *cut wages*. This was the situation which led to the strike of 1926.

4. Formation of trade unions

In 1889, a Miners' Federation of Great Britain was formed with a view to improving wages, working conditions and safety in the mines. It also aimed to bring about the *8-hour day* and successfully achieved this in 1908.

From 1910–1914, there was a lot of unrest in the coal mines as they fought for a *national minimum wage* in their industry. Despite massive strikes, they did not get this. However, during the war, the Government took control of the mines and gave a national wage. After the war, ownership of the mines was returned to the coal owners.

(b) In the early 1920s, the price of coal fell and mine owners began to lower wages. This led to a major strike, in 1926, which eventually ended in failure. During the twenties and thirties, unemployment in the industry rose as colliery owners closed mines during the depression.

5. Government Invervention

Working conditions changed as a result of Government legislation.

   (i) *1842* — children under the age of ten and all females were forbidden to work underground.

  (ii) *1862* — single shaft mines were declared illegal.

 (iii) *1872* — mine managers had to have a certificate to prove they could do the job.

 (iv) *1909* — eight-hour working day was introduced.

7

Changes in Employment and Working Conditions on the Land

The Effect of Population Growth and Urbanisation on Agriculture

1. *More land* had to be brought under cultivation to increase food production. This was done by draining and enclosing new land.

2. *New methods* had to be introduced to produce more food, e.g. new crops like the potato and new crop rotations.

3. *New technology* made farming more efficient.

4. The arrival of the *Irish* provided seasonal labour.

5. There was a *"golden age of agriculture"* from 1846–1876 as the increased demand for food brought prosperity to farming.

6. By the end of the 19th century, Britain was *importing cheap foreign food* from abroad, most notably America. In 1914, on the outbreak of World War One, Britain imported about two-thirds of her food supplies.

The Workforce

(a) In 1830, more people were employed in agriculture than any other industry. The 1851 census showed that in Scotland one in every three working men were employed directly in agriculture.

By the end of the 19th century, the numbers working in agriculture stood at around 200 000, but by 1931 this figure had fallen to 160 000.

(b) Children made up some of the workforce in 1830 when schooling was not compulsory. After 1872, children had to attend school by law although many stayed off school when it came to harvest time and at other busy times in the farming year.

(c) Women also made up a large amount of the workforce, approximately 25% of those employed worked on the land in 1880. Employers were keen to take on women since they could be paid lower wages than men.

Women were used to labour on the farms, just like men, with the exception of actually ploughing. They were also used to work in the farmhouse.

During World War One, women made up the Land Army to keep production going at a time when men were conscripted into the army.

After World War One, the low pay of farming and the new opportunities of office work persuaded many to seek new types of employment.

(d) Irish families provided a seasonal workforce throughout the period, particularly at harvest time.

(e) Workers tended to move from one farm to another in search of better conditions. In order to get farmwork, people had to attend a 'feeing fair' when the workers would reach an agreement about wages and conditions with the farmer.

Working Conditions

(i) *Accidents* — The development of new technology brought more accidents on the farm. The threshing machine, for example, which replaced the flail, was in widespread use in the 1850s but was often the cause of accidents.

(ii) *Men* had to work long hours for *low wages*. For example, a *horseman* was vital to the working of the farm throughout most of the period. At the busiest time of the year he would start work at about 4.00 a.m. and finish about 7.00 p.m.

(iii) *Motorised power* — By 1914, motorised tractors were sufficiently light to signal a real breakthrough in farming technology. The arrival of the tractor and motorised power signalled the beginning of the end for the horsemen and the blacksmiths. Not all farmers could afford to purchase a tractor and continued to use horse power. The figures below indicate the extent of the decline in horse power:

Year	1839	1895	1918	1939
No. of horses in thousands	1500	1545	1337	987

(iv) **Wages and accommodation**

Wages were *low* even at times when farming prospered. Accommodation was *basic* even though in some parts of the countryside cottages were substantially improved.

(v) **Formation of trade unions**

Trade unions were slow to develop and give the farm workers any protection. Joseph Arch formed an *Agricultural Labourers' Union* in 1872 to achieve higher pay and better working conditions. In Scotland, a similar organisation, the *Scottish Farm Servants Union* was formed but made no progress in improving conditions.

(vi) **Government intervention**

It was not until 1937 that *unemployment insurance* was introduced for agriculture.

8

Health in Urban and Rural Areas

Living conditions in the towns were unhealthy to such an extent that life expectancy was about half that of someone living in the countryside. This was shown very clearly in the 1842 Chadwick Report on the 'Sanitary Conditions of the Labouring Population' which compared the rural area of Rutland to the industrial town of Manchester.

	Rutland	*Manchester*
Worker — average age of death	38	17
Gentry — average age of death	52	38

The figures above show that while conditions in the countryside were not good, they were better than in the towns. Drinking water was not contaminated, excrement was removed and houses were spread out so that disease did not spread so quickly.

The Main Killer Diseases of the 19th Century

(i) *Tuberculosis* — Accounted for one-third of all deaths from disease in the 19th century.

(ii) *Typhus* — In 1870s, typhus averaged 1400 deaths a year.

(iii) *Cholera* — Major epidemics in 1831–1832, 1848–1849, 1853–1854, 1866–1867.

(iv) *Scarlet Fever* — Ninety-five per cent of cases were children under ten and about one child in every five who contacted it died.

(v) *Typhoid* — Where there was an inadequate water supply, this disease flourished.

(vi) *Smallpox* — Although vaccination was made compulsory in 1853, the vaccine was poorly administered.

Social Conditions Leading to Disease, 1830–1900

(i) *Overcrowding in slum housing* — The rapid growth of towns caused a terrible housing problem. In Scotland, this was particularly true of Central Glasgow and Greenock as the table below shows:

Year	Town	Number of People per acre
1881	Glasgow (central)	1000
1881	Greenock (central)	470
1881	Liverpool	300
1881	Edinburgh	55

As a result, more people in Scotland stayed in one-roomed homes than in England. The figures below for Glasgow in 1901 show the clear connection between overcrowding and disease:

Type of Accomodation	Death Rate per Thousand
1 room	32·7
2 rooms	21·3
3 rooms	13·7
4 rooms	11·2

(ii) *Inadequate water supply* — Water pumps in the street often supplied water which contained impurities which led to disease. The cholera epidemics in particular were caused by this.

(iii) *Adulterated food* — Colouring was added to milk which was no longer fresh to make it look creamy. In 1877, a quarter of all milk examined was found to be adulterated. It was not until about 1900 that milk was sterilized.

(iv) *Lack of proper sewage* — Cesspools were unable to cope with the demands of an increased population, with the result that they often became choked and contaminated nearby wells. There was some improvement in the second half of the 19th century when cities like Edinburgh introduced a pail collection system. Householders would be fined if they did not have their pails ready on collection day. It was not until the end of the 19th century that water-borne sewerage schemes were introduced in the major cities of Britain.

(v) *Bad working conditions* — *(a)* long hours
(b) unprotected machines
(c) little regard to health and safety.

(vi) *Poverty* — This was caused when:
(a) Families were large and wages were low;
(b) The wage earner became unemployed or ill and could not bring in a wage to support his family.
Although *poorhouses* were created in Scotland after the 1845 Poor Law Amendment Act to give a basic provision for the poor, elderly and infirm, many people put up with extreme hardship to avoid going into the poorhouse.

(vii) *Lack of medical knowledge* — There was little knowledge of medicine, although hospitals benefited enormously from the work of Simpson and Lister in being able to carry out successful operations in a painless manner and with every chance of recovery:
1847 — Chloroform first used as an anaesthetic
1865 — Antiseptic surgery was introduced in Glasgow by Joseph Lister.

Government Intervention in Public Health, 1830–1900

The Government passed two pieces of legislation to tackle the problem of public health. These Acts gave local councils the power to improve social conditions.

1848 — *Public Health Act*

(a) Local Authorities were to set up Health Boards if the death rate was over 23 per 1000, or 10% of the people asked for it.

(b) Local Health Boards were given the power to appoint medical officers of health, provide clean water and proper drainage, clean, pave and light streets.

N.B. There was no compulsion in this Act and it was not that effective.

1875 — *Public Health Act* — This Act compelled local authorities to

(a) Provide adequate sewerage, drainage and water supply.

(b) Report infectious diseases to the Medical Officer.

(c) Maintain, pave and light streets.

Glasgow serves as a good example of how these Acts gave councils the power to improve social conditions. Other councils, particularly Edinburgh and Dundee, were not far behind in tackling their own problems in a similar way:

Glasgow

(i) A *new reservoir* was started at Loch Katrine in the Trossachs in 1855. As a result, only 53 people died from cholera in the 1865–1866 epidemic.

(ii) A *Medical Officer of Health* was appointed in 1863.

(iii) Systematic *destruction of slum property* started in 1866. As a result, 30,000 people had been evicted by 1885 and their houses destroyed.

(iv) *Gas supply* was provided by the council at half the previous price in 1867.

(v) The first municipal (council) *fever hospital* was opened in 1869.

(vi) *Wash houses* and public baths were introduced in 1878.

(vii) A modern *sewer system* was introduced in 1893.

Reasons for Decline in Specific Diseases, 1830–1900

(a) *Improvements in Living Conditions*

Tuberculosis — Due to an improvement in *diet* and a *fresher supply of milk* in particular, there was a 50% reduction in death through the disease between 1850 and 1900. Nonetheless, TB remained the second greatest killer disease, next to heart disease.

Typhus — Better *water supply* resulted in improved personal hygiene which, in turn, reduced the spread of the disease through contact with the louse. Better *diet* also contributed to greater resistance to the disease.

Typhoid — Better *water supply* brought about better sanitary arrangements. By 1904, the death rate was one third of what it had been in 1870.

Cholera — Wiped out by the end of the century due to better *water supply*.

Dysentry and Diarrhoea — Better *water supply* and *food* brought about a reduction in death from bowel infections.

(b) *Medical Improvements*

Smallpox — Once vaccination was made compulsory and fully enforced after 1871, all infants were vaccinated and the disease virtually disappeared.

(c) *Change in nature of disease*

Scarlet Fever — During the second half of the 19th century, death from scarlet fever fell by 81%. This was mainly due to a *biological change* in the nature of the disease, which made it less deadly, and the introduction of *isolated fever hospitals*.

Further Improvement in Health, 1900–1939

Despite the improvements in social conditions brought about by council intervention, the level of poverty which existed in Britain in 1900 remained high and this contributed to ill health. Research by Charles Booth (1889) and Seebohm Rowntree (1901) in London and York showed that 30% of those living in towns were below the poverty line. As a result of these findings and the army's rejection, due to their poor physical condition, of one in three of the volunteers who wanted to enlist for the Boer War (1899–1902), political parties started to look at ways of overcoming poverty. The Liberal Government of 1906–1911 did much to improve social conditions and give support to those most at risk — the elderly, young, ill and unemployed.

(a) *The old*

In 1908, old age pensions of five shillings a week for all single persons aged 70 or over was introduced.

(b) *The young*

In 1906, the School Meals Act gave authorities the power to provide school meals and made them free for the poorest.
In 1907, the Medical Inspection Act introduced the regular school medical inspection.

(c) The ill

A National Insurance scheme was introduced in 1911 whereby insured workers received money for up to 26 weeks if they were off work through illness.

(d) The unemployed

A National Insurance scheme was introduced in 1911 to cover workers in the building, shipyard, labouring and engineering industries.

Conclusion

Health in urban and rural areas improved considerably between 1830–1939. This was due to improvements in social conditions brought about by:

(i) Town councils tackling the problems of slum housing, water supply and sanitation.

(ii) Central government tackling the problem of poverty through reforms started between 1906 and 1911.

(iii) Better food supply brought about by a combination of the railway network, bringing fresh food to the towns, and Co-operative shops providing good food at a fair price. (The first Co-op was opened at Rochdale in 1844, and the Scottish Co-operative Wholesale Society was formed in 1869.)

(iv) A rise in real wages for the working class, who could buy better clothes, shoes, furniture and food.

(v) Better medical provision through hospitals using anaesthetics and antiseptics. After 1858, all doctors had to be fully qualified.

N.B. People living in the countryside were healthier than townsfolk due to a better diet.

9

Housing in Urban and Rural Areas

Urban Housing

In 1830, the main features of urban housing were:

1. *One-roomed houses* — This was particularly bad in the large towns of Glasgow, Edinburgh and Aberdeen, but was a feature of housing for the poorest in every town. Most houses only had one room which acted as a

sitting, eating and sleeping room. At least one in every three families in Scotland lived in a *one-roomed house*.

2. *Absence of toilets* — Most of the population had to use either buckets or outside privies (toilets) which frequently drained into a cesspit or open drain. Waste was often left in the open or dumped into the river. Greenock was one of Scotland's dirtiest towns with large open refuse dumps.

3. *No water supply* — Most people collected their water in buckets from a stand pipe in the street. The water was frequently impure and led to diseases such as cholera.

4. *Slum Housing* — Old hovels hardly fit for human habitation existed in most towns.

5. *New Back-to-back Housing* — These were houses built as cheaply as possible to house the factory workers. Although they were new, the privy was outside the house and shared; ventilation was poor, houses were too small.

Improvements in Housing by 1939

The gradual intervention of both local and central government led to a substantial improvement in housing by the end of the period for some of the working class.

1855 — *Nuisance Removal Act* — Allowed local authorities in towns over 200 000 to carry out the compulsory purchase of insanitary houses.

1909 — *Housing and Town Planning Act* — Allowed local authorities to prepare 'town planning' schemes.

1919 — *Addison's Housing Act* — Attempted to tackle the house shortage made worse during the war years when little building took place. Unfortunately, 'homes fit for heroes' failed to fully materialise as government money for housing ran out in 1921.

1924 — *Wheatley's Housing Act* — Led to a considerable building programme by local authorities of council houses. These houses had electricity, indoor toilets and gardens. Although the poorest of the working class could not afford the rent, they did provide good quality housing at a reasonable rent.

1930 — *Greenwood's Housing Act* — Paved the way for large scale slum clearance.

By the end of the period the features of urban housing were:

(i) Very few Scottish houses had only one room. By 1914, only 13% of all Scottish houses had one room compared to 34% in 1861.

(ii) Most houses had indoor toilets.

(iii) Most houses had piped water and baths.

(iv) Slums still existed but the very worst had been removed.

(v) Low-rise, detached, three storey tenement blocks appeared, during the inter-war years (1919–1939), on the outskirts of towns where land was cheap.

(vi) Private housing produced a variety of styles, from the grand Victorian mansions to the 2/3 roomed flat, to the inter-war bungalows.

(vii) Electricity was introduced to most houses between the wars.

(viii) There was still an absence of cheap rented accommodation for poor working-class families.

N.B. In comparison to England, Scotland had less private housing and more council housing. English houses also had more rooms than most Scottish houses.

Rural Housing

There were different types of rural housing and most were very basic.

(a) *Cottages* — Most had thatched roofs up until the end of the 19th century and were a lot later in getting tapped water, baths, indoor sanitation and electricity than the cities.

(b) *Black houses* — In the Western Isles, these houses consisted of a living area and an area to keep the cattle. There was no chimney and smoke escaped from a hole in the roof.

(c) *Bothies* — Farm workers stayed in these houses, which were very basic. Bothies were found in Angus and further south. Frequently, bothies were rooms over stables and had precious little furniture.

(d) *Chaumers* — Farm workers in the area of Aberdeen stayed in basic bed accommodation and went to the farm kitchen for their meals.

(e) *Miners' cottages* — These houses were reasonable although they were badly overcrowded. They were built in rows.

Despite some improvements in rural housing throughout the 19th century, the Royal Commission on Housing in 1917 showed that terrible conditions still existed:

(i) Black houses were decaying in the Hebrides.
(ii) Damp earthern floors existed on Lowland estates.
(iii) Open sewers ran between rows of miners' cottages.

10

Parliamentary Reform in Scotland and England

Background

Prior to 1832 and the Reform Act of that year, Britain was not a very democratic country.

(i) *A limited franchise* — Very few people in Britain had the vote and they were wealthy landowners.

(ii) *Poor distribution of seats* — Some constituencies, particularly in the south of England, returned Members of Parliament where nobody lived at a time when new large towns with many people, like Manchester, had no M.P.

(iii) *System of voting* — Led to bribery, intimidation and corruption taking place at election time.

From 1830–1939 there was a trend towards making Britain's Government more democratic by

(i) *Extending the franchise* — Giving more people the vote by Acts of Parliament in 1832, 1867, 1884, 1918 and 1928.

(ii) *Redistributing the constituencies* so that eventually they would be of near equal size.

(iii) *System of voting* to be secret.

1832 Reform Act

This Act was passed by the *Whigs* despite strong opposition from the *Tories*.

(i) *The franchise* — The Act turned out to be a big disappointment for the working class, which had clamoured for the vote. The vote was carefully given to the £10 householder, i.e. people from the middle classes who were shopkeepers, and not the working class.

(ii) *Redistribution of seats* — Many of the old rotten boroughs like Old Sarum lost two M.Ps and the new industrial towns received one or two according to their size, e.g. large towns like Manchester, Leeds and Blackburn were given two M.Ps while towns like Bury, Rochdale and

Walsall were given one M.P. However, sizes of constituencies were not equal.

(iii) *System of voting* — The open system of voting remained unchanged.

The Second Reform Act, 1867

This Act was passed by the Tories who were led by Benjamin Disraeli. The terms of the Act were:

(a) Extension of the franchise — The working class in the boroughs were given the vote.

(b) Redistribution of seats — The small boroughs with a population under 10 000 lost one of the two seats — the counties received 25 extra M.Ps — Scotland's number of Members of Parliament rose from 53 to 60.

Assessment of the 1867 Act

(a) This Act extended the franchise even more than the 1832 Act by almost *doubling the electorate*. It had an enormous impact on the numbers who now had the vote in the towns.

	Pre-1867	After 1867
Glasgow	18 000	47 000
Leeds	7 217	35 510
Newcastle	6 630	21 407

(b) The Act was passed by the Tory Government, who attempted to 'dish the Whigs' after the Whigs had failed to get Parliament to pass a similar measure of reform in 1866. At the time it was thought to have been a *massive gamble* by the Tory leader, Benjamin Disraeli, in giving so many of the working class the vote as these new voters might well vote for the Whigs and keep the Tories for ever in opposition. For this reason, the 1867 Act was called a *'leap in the dark'*. As it turned out, the Tories did lose the next election but won the election of 1874.

(c) There still remained a *need to redistribute the seats* as the South of England was still over represented.

Third Reform Act, 1884

This Act was passed by William Ewart Gladstone's Liberal Party. The terms of the Act were:

(a) Extension of the franchise — This gave the vote to the male working class in the counties.

(b) Redistribution of seats (1885) — Boroughs with less than 1500 inhabitants lost both M.Ps, while those with less than 50 000 inhabitants lost one M.P. Scotland's number of M.Ps rose from 60 to 72.

Assessment of the 1884 Act

(a) *Extension of the franchise* — Although about another two million men were added and almost doubled the electorate, it was only householders who could vote. As many as 40% of men could not vote because they were not householders — women were totally excluded from voting.

(b) *Redistribution of seats* — At last seats were distributed throughout the country on an equitable basis. On average, one M.P. represented about 54 000 people.

11

The Suffragette Movement and Votes for Women

Reasons for the Rise of the Suffragette Movement

(a) Women were totally excluded from the political system in Britain at a time when countries like Iceland gave women the vote.

(b) Many women were better educated than the men who were enfranchised by the Acts of 1867 and 1884.

(c) Women had few legal rights and many of the working class women worked in sweated industries with long hours, low wages and dreadful working conditions. Without having the vote, women were helpless to improve this situation.

(d) Peaceful suffragist societies had unsuccessfully campaigned for votes for women since 1870 but neither political party would risk giving women the vote.

Formation of the Woman's Social and Political Union

Formed — 1903 by the widow of a Manchester barrister, Mrs. Emmeline Pankhurst.

Leader — Emmeline and her daughters, Sylvia and Christabel, formed a strong autocratic leadership.

Supporters — Largely middle-class women.

Motto — Deeds not words.

Methods

1. *Marches* and processions.
2. *Propaganda.*
3. *Disrupting meetings* held by Liberal politicians and interrupting debates in the House of Commons from the Public Gallery.
4. *Physically attacking* leading politicians, e.g. Asquith attacked in Lossiemouth.
5. *Smashing windows.*
6. *Setting post boxes on fire* or pouring acid into the pillar boxes to destroy the letters.
7. *Slashing paintings* in art galleries.
8. *Chaining themselves* to the railings of Buckingham Palace and Downing Street.
9. *Arson* — Setting fire to buildings such as Ayr Race Course stand in 1914.
10. Going on *hunger strike* when imprisoned.

N.B. These were methods designed to gain publicity. Possibly the incident of 1913, when *Emily Davison* died from injuries as a result of running in front of the King's horse at the Epsom Derby, gained most publicity.

Government Response

(a) The Prime Minister, Herbert Asquith, was not in favour of giving women the vote. He feared that women would vote Conservative.

(b) Government first of all 'force-fed' suffragettes who went on hunger strike.

(c) In 1913, the Government bowed to public opinion and ended forced-feeding. They passed the 'Temporary Discharge of Prisoners Act' which allowed the release of those who were on hunger strikes for a period until they had recovered and then they would be rearrested. This became known as the 'Cat and Mouse Act'.

Suffragettes — Success or Failure

(a) Many supporters of 'votes for women' left the movement because they were appalled by the use of violence.

(b) The Suffragettes abandoned their militant tactics in 1914, when the war began, and gave their support to the war effort.

(c) In 1918, women gained the vote largely as the result of the fine work women had carried out during the war, e.g. munition workers, transport, nursing, farming.

The Representation of the People Act (June 1918)

This extended the franchise by giving the vote to:

(a) All men over 21,

(b) All women over 30.

1928 Act

This gave the vote to all women on the same basis as men.

Summary

The period 1830–1939 witnessed the *growth of democracy* in Britain. In 1830, there was a limited franchise (few people could vote), an unequal distribution of constituencies (many large industrial towns had no M.P.) and a system of voting which led to bribery, intimidation and corruption.

By 1939, these three failings of the 1830 system had been overcome. The fight for the vote at times bordered on a revolution as groups took to the streets and rioted. The working class, the Chartists, and the suffragettes all caused major problems for the Government in maintaining the law.

The vote came in piecemeal fashion with the middle-class winning the vote in 1832; the working class in the boroughs in 1867; the working class in the counties in 1884; women over 30 in 1918 and women over 21 in 1928.

As more people received the vote, it became impossible to bribe electors since it would be too costly. When the Secret Ballot was introduced, in 1872, intimidation at elections was eliminated.

The redistribution of seats also progressed in a piecemeal fashion so that by 1884 each constituency represented about the same number of people.

By the end of the period, Britain was a far more democratic country than when it had started.

Political parties had to respond to this growth in the electorate and become better organised. The Whig party became the Liberal Party and the Tory party the Conservative Party. A third political party, the Labour Party, was formed in 1900 and had sufficient electoral support to form the first Labour Government in 1923. In 1929, Labour again formed another Government. The Labour Party, supported by the trade unions, replaced the Liberal Party as the main opposition party to the Conservative Party by the end of the period.

Between 1830 and 1939, political change had been achieved and groups which were excluded from the political system in 1830, the *middle class*, the *working class* and *women*, were enfranchised and their interests represented in Parliament.

UNIT 1 — Changing Life in Scotland and Britain

CONTEXT C: 1880s to Present Day

1

Population Growth and Distribution

Population Growth

	Scotland	Britain
1881	3·73 million	37 million
1931	4·84 million	45 million
1951	5·09 million	50 million
1981	5·13 million	55 million

Reasons for Population Growth

Between 1880 and 1990 there was a big rise in the population of Scotland and Britain. A dramatic fall in the death rate more than made up for a fall in the birth rate during this period.

Period	Birth Rate		Death Rate	
	Scotland	Britain	Scotland	Britain
1871–1880	34·9	35·4	21·6	21·4
1901–1910	28·4	27·3	16·3	15·4
1931–1940	17·8	14·8	13·3	12·3
1961–1965	19·7	18·1	12·2	11·8

Reasons for the Fall in the Birth Rate

(i) *Marriage and employment* — After 1880, more people were able to continue their education through technical training or higher education. From the late 1950s, more women opted to continue their careers. People married later and couples postponed having a family.

(ii) *Developments in contraception* — Contraceptive devices were available to men and women in 1880. However, they became more widely used among all classes in society in the 1920s as a result of the pioneering work of Dr. Marie Stopes, who opened family planning clinics in London. These soon spread to other parts of the country.

In the 1960s, the contraceptive pill became available and free contraception was given under the National Health Service.

(iii) *Changing attitudes* — As people strived for more affluence they tended to have smaller families

      1880s   Average family = 6 children
      1930s   Average family = 4 children
      1980s   Average family = 2·2 children.

Reasons for Fall in Death Rate

(i) *Better diet* — Improvements in agricultural methods and food transport meant that more people enjoyed a healthier diet. For much of the 20th century, Britain enjoyed the benefits of cheap food imported from abroad, from the British Empire and the Commonwealth.

(ii) *Better medical care* — The death rate from disease continued to fall sharply after 1880. The development of vaccination, anti-biotics (1940s) and innovations in surgery contributed to this.

(iii) *Improvements in hygiene, sanitation and water supply* — Improvements in water supply and cheaper fuel have encouraged cleanliness and better hygiene in the home.

(iv) *Better housing* — Steps taken towards slum clearance and construction of better homes improved living conditions.

(v) *Improvements in welfare* — Government intervention to ease poverty, e.g. old age pensions, National Insurance, school meals.

In 1880, a person would be expected to live to the age of 43. By 1990, a person could be expected to live to the age of 78.

Redistribution of Population

1. Growth of towns

	1881	*1931*	*1981*
Aberdeen	105 000	170 000	214 000
Dundee	140 000	176 000	181 000
Edinburgh	295 000	439 000	441 000
Glasgow	587 000	1 088 000	747 000

Reasons for Greater Increase of Population in Urban Areas

(i) *Decline in employment in agriculture* — Changes in farming methods and mechanisation meant a decrease in rural employment.

Percentage of population working in agriculture
1881	13·5%
1931	7·0%
1981	2·0%

(ii) *The development of industry* has encouraged people to come to towns and cities to seek employment.

(iii) *Cultural changes* have led many people in rural areas to see life in towns as being more desirable — nearer to shops and recreation.

2

Immigration to Scotland

1880–1918

The main immigrant groups during this period were:

(i) *Irish*

Immigration from Ireland had an important impact on many parts of Scotland in the 19th century. However, the number of Irish immigrants decreased after 1880.

Number of Irish-born inhabitants in Scotland

1881 — 218 745
1921 — 159 020
1931 — 124 296

(ii) *Eastern Europeans*

There was massive emigration from the Baltic States during this period. Six thousand Lithuanians settled in Scotland, mainly in the mining areas of Lanarkshire.

Eastern European Jews fleeing persecution also arrived in Scotland, The Gorbals, in Glasgow, had a community of over 5000 Jews by 1914.

(iii) *Italians*

Around 4000 people, escaping the poverty of southern Italy, arrived in Scotland between 1890 and 1914.

1918–1939

Immigration decreased during the years of the depression. Some Jews, escaping persecution in Germany, arrived in Scotland in the 1930s.

1939–1990

In the 1950s, the Government encouraged immigrants from the British Commonwealth. Indians, Pakistanis, Afro-Caribbeans and Hong Kong Chinese arrived to take up employment. Although these groups settled mainly in the more prosperous south of Britain, communities did appear in Scotland. An Asian community of around 50 000 people developed in central Scotland.

Government immigration controls since 1962 have reduced immigration from the Commonwealth.

3

Emigration from Scotland

Many Scots left to escape the lack of opportunities created by economic hardship. Countries like Australia, New Zealand and Canada encouraged people to seek new lives in their countries. They placed advertisements in local newspapers offering employment and assistance with fares.

1880–1939

Numbers of people emigrating from Scotland

    1882 — 32 000
    1912 — 72 000
    1922 — 87 000
    1932 — 6 000

The peak periods for emigration usually occurred during times of economic hardship. However, emigration fell during the 1930s because the depression affected most of the world. Emigration during the period was highest from rural areas — especially the Highlands and Islands.

1945–1990

Estimated loss of population through emigration

    1931–1951 — 249 000
    1951–1961 — 255 000
    1961–1971 — 195 000

In the 1950s and early 1960s, some Scots sought new lives in Australia, New Zealand and Canada while the assisted passages scheme continued.

The 'Brain Drain'

Although there was less opportunity for unskilled workers to emigrate to Commonwealth countries during the 1960s and 1970s, many skilled workers and professional people left Scotland to work in other countries, especially in North America, where they were offered better pay and conditions.

Many Scots have moved south of the border to seek education and employment. By 1980, it was estimated that 12% of people born in Scotland lived in England and Wales.

4

Technological Change and its Effect on Developments in Shipbuilding

1880–1918

British shipbuilders took a lead in introducing new technology, especially on the Clyde.

(i) The first steel hulled, ocean-going ship was launched on the Clyde in 1879.

(ii) Steam engines — Parson's steam turbine was pioneered by Clyde engineers.

(iii) The Clyde was ideally suited for the production of steel built steamships — raw materials, engineering expertise, labour all close at hand.

During this period British shipbuilding led the world. In 1900, Britain built 80% of the world's ships. However, despite Britain's dominant position during this period, foreign competition began to appear. The first diesel powered vessel was launched in Denmark in 1911. Shipbuilding in Germany was developing quickly, making use of the latest methods of production.

1918–1939

The 1920s and early 1930s saw a slump in shipbuilding. Production in British yards fell from 2·5 million tons in 1920 to 0·7 million tons in 1930.

Reasons

(i) *Foreign competition* — In Europe and the U.S.A., new technology was adopted. Welding replaced riveting, diesel turbines were introduced,

(ii) *Resistance to new technology* — Many British yards were owned by small family companies, e.g. Stephen's on the Clyde, Hunter's on the Tyne. These companies often could not afford to introduce new technology. They tended to be cautious and were not inclined to experiment with new methods.

Shipyard workers also resisted new techniques for fear of job losses.

(iii) *Lack of Government support* — Unlike the governments of many of Britain's competitors, the British Government gave little support to shipbuilding.

(iv) *Lack of demand* — Decline in demand for passenger liners and the effects of naval disarmament during peacetime severely affected British yards.

Technological Improvements

Technological change during this period was very limited when compared with other countries. However, the pneumatic riveter was introduced in many shipyards, larger cranes were used and more use was made of electrical power.

1939–1990

The Second World War gave a boost to British shipyards, which continued into the 1950s, while some of Britain's competitors, e.g. Germany and Japan, rebuilt their industry after the devastation caused by wartime bombing. However, there were few technological advances in British yards during this period. Some more machine tools were introduced and there was more electrification and larger cranes.

In the 1960s and 1970s, a steady decline took place in British shipbuilding.

Reasons

(i) *Foreign Competition* — Britain's competitors, U.S.A., Japan, Germany, Scandinavia and Korea, introduced the latest technology, including enclosed yards where work could continue all year round regardless of weather conditions. They introduced assembly line methods which allowed ships to be built quickly and cheaply.

(ii) *Lack of new technology* — Even in the prosperous years, shipyard owners did not invest in new technology. As a result, British yards got a bad reputation for high costs and late delivery.

Many British yards were in confined spaces close on river banks hemmed in by houses and factories. This made it more difficult to change the layout and increase the size of the shipyards to allow manufacture on a larger scale.

(iii) *Poor Industrial Relations* — A long history of mutual distrust and resentment between employers and workers contributed to many strikes over pay and conditions during this period. Attempts by management to introduce new labour-saving methods and tools often led to 'demarcation disputes'.

(iv) *Government assistance* — The Government gave some assistance to the shipbuilding industry but did not subsidise the industry to the same extent as shipbuilding was helped abroad. This led to British yards falling further behind their competitors in introducing new technology. The industry was nationalised in 1977 but, under Mrs. Thatcher's Government, after 1979, profitable yards were sold off whilst others closed.

5

Technological Change and its Effects on Developments in Road Transport

1880–1918

This period saw the beginning of motorised road transport.

(i) *Motor carriages* — The first motor carriages appeared on Britain's roads in the 1880s. They were hand built by skilled craftsmen in small workshops. They were the expensive playthings of wealthy enthusiasts.

(ii) *Trams* — Electrical power and the adaptation of railway technology led to replacement of horse drawn omnibuses by electric trams. By 1918, most Scottish towns had a tram system.

(iii) *Motor buses* — The development of more reliable engines allowed the development of motor buses. Some motorbus companies operated over short distances between towns and suburbs. SMT was founded in 1905. However, the railway remained the main method of travel between towns.

1918–1939

There were major changes in motor vehicle manufacture during this period.

(i) War-time improvements in the internal combustion engine and mass production were applied to motor manufacture. The assembly line techniques of the American manufacturer, Henry Ford, were introduced to Britain. Ford opened his first assembly line in Manchester before the First World War. His techniques were copied by British companies such as Morris and Austin. As a result of this, the number of cars produced in Britain increased dramatically and the price of a family car dropped from around £200 in 1922 to £100 in 1935.

(ii) Motoring remained a method of transport for the better off. By 1939, one family in eight had a car.

(iii) Improved technology also benefited the motorbus industry. Large motorbus companies grew across Scotland, e.g. W. Alexander (Falkirk).

Army buses from the war were bought up cheaply by bus companies, allowing them to expand their services.

(iv) Trams remained the main form of city transport. There were 1200 trams running in Glasgow in 1939.

(v) The increase in motorised road transport led the Government to introduce some safety measures:

      1926 — Traffic lights introduced;
      1930 — Compulsory driving tests and licenses for bus drivers;
      1934 — Cats-eyes introduced;
             Pedestrian crossings;
      1935 — Compulsory driving tests for all motorists;
             30 mph speed limit in towns.

1939–1990

Further technological improvements contributed to a boom in motor transport during this period.

The Motoring Boom

Year	Number of cars	Year	Number of lorries
1945	1·7 million	1945	0·49 million
1955	4·6 million	1955	1·14 million
1965	8·4 million	1971	1·6 million
1975	13·5 million	1986	1·7 million
1986	18·8 million		

By 1989, 80% of freight was carried by road.

45

Improvements in technology contributed to a major increase in number of road vehicles during this period. This led to major changes in road transport.

(i) Government had to take steps to ease traffic problems caused by the boom in road transport

     Motorways — First section of motorway in Britain was built in 1958. The first in Scotland was opened in 1964.

     By-passes — New roads were built to carry traffic away from town centres. For example, all main towns on A75 Euroroute between Stranraer and Gretna were by-passed by 1990.

     Bridges — Large bridges were constructed to shorten travelling distances and ease traffic on certain roads. The Forth Road Bridge was completed in 1964 and the Tay Road Bridge 1966.

(ii) Steps had also been taken to ease traffic congestion in towns
— trams had disappeared by 1962
— parking restrictions, ring roads and by-passes had been introduced.

(iii) The steady increase in the number of road vehicles led the Government to introduce more road safety measures.

Speed Limits

1896	15 mph
1903	20 mph
1935	30 mph
1967	70 mph
1967	Breathalyser introduced
1983	Seat belts compulsory for front seat passengers.

(iv) Car manufacturers took steps to improve the safety of vehicles, e.g. strengthened passenger compartments, collapsible steering columns.

6

Changes in Housing in Rural and Urban Areas

Housing in Urban Areas

1880–1918

Industrialisation brought thousands of people into the cities in search of work. This often led to overcrowding and slum conditions.

The main features of housing at this time were:

(i) People who came to the towns to find work rented homes from their employers or other private builders.

(ii) In England, rows of back-to-back two-storey houses were common.

(iii) In Scotland, high land prices encouraged builders to put up four to six storey tenements. These contained one-roomed (single-ends) or two-roomed (room and kitchen) apartments.

(iv) Some improvements did take place in the late 19th century. The 1875 Public Health Act led to improvements in water supply and sewerage. By 1890, there were 100 miles of sewers under Glasgow's streets and water was piped into the city from Loch Katrine.

(v) Even in well built housing with improved sanitation, overcrowding led to unhealthy conditions.
In 1911, 50% of Scots lived in one- or two-roomed accommodation.

1918–1939

During this period, the Government intervened in housing. A number of Housing Acts were passed which led local councils to clear slums and build new housing.

(i) *Housing and Planning Act 1919* (Addison Act)
Required local authorities with more than 20 000 inhabitants to build cheap rented accommodation. Government subsidies were provided. Three hundred and twelve thousand homes were built under this Act, 25 500 in Scotland. Many good quality homes were built but they tended to be expensive to rent.

This scheme was abandoned as part of Government spending cuts in 1921.

(ii) *Chamberlain's Housing Act 1923*
This encouraged private house building with Government subsidies. This scheme benefited those who could afford to buy their own homes.

(iii) *The Wheatley Housing Act 1924*
The first Labour Government aimed to build 2·5 million new homes. A substantial subsidy was given to councils and 0·5 million new homes were built before the subsidies were cut in 1933. Council housing remained beyond the reach of the lower paid.

(iv) *The Greenwood Act 1930*
This forced local authorities to take steps to remove slums. Two hundred and forty-five thousand slums were demolished by 1939. However, over half a million slums still remained.

1939–1990

The new Labour Government of 1945 faced a severe housing shortage. Half a million homes had been destroyed by German bombing and house building stopped during the war years. The Government was determined to tackle housing problems but a shortage of building materials after the war delayed progress.

Attempts to solve housing problems

(i) *1940s — Prefabricated houses*
Made from factory-built concrete sections, they could be erected quickly on site. They appeared in most Scottish towns. Edinburgh local authority put up 4000. Glasgow Housing Corporation built 3000 'prefabs'. Many people who were rehoused in prefabs were very happy with these detached homes with modern facilities — bathrooms, toilets, gardens etc.

Prefabricated housing was a limited, short term response to desperate need.

(ii) *1946 New Towns Act*
Many new homes were built in the 'new towns' built outside the great industrial conurbations. By 1963, 18 new towns had been built in Britain, including Cumbernauld, Glenrothes, Livingston, East Kilbride and Irvine.

Housing in the new towns was often carefully designed with shops, schools, leisure facilities and factories within easy reach.

(iii) *1950s–1960s Council Housing schemes*
Between 1955 and 1968, 800 000 slum dwellings were cleared and two million people were resettled in new council homes.

Large estates appeared on the edge of major cities. Although these schemes succeeded in rehousing thousands of former slum dwellers, the estates very often had no shops, pubs or leisure facilities. The tenement communities were broken up. Vandalism and violent crime became a problem in many of these estates. Tenants did their best to escape. For example, by 1980 a quarter of the homes in the Glasgow schemes of Castlemilk and Drumchapel lay empty.

(iv) *Housing in the 1980s*

Under the Conservative Government, councils were encouraged to sell off council houses. There was a boom in private ownership during this period. By 1984, more than half of Britain's homes were privately owned.

Housing in Rural Areas

Before 1880

Standards of housing were generally poor. Many rural workers lived in cottages that they had built for themselves. For example, in the Highlands and islands black houses were still common. These were small stone-built houses with earthen floors shared with the animals. Standards of sanitation were basic and they were often affected by damp. Unmarried male farm workers were often accomodated in rough outbuildings called bothies.

Changes in Rural Housing 1880–1990

Standards of housing saw a general improvement during this period.

Reasons

(i) Landowners had to improve standards of housing in order to try and keep workers from leaving the land. Cottages were improved and bothies were very rare by 1918.

(ii) After 1918, the Government made grants available for the improvement of rural housing. Tenants could obtain assistance for installing proper sanitation, indoor toilets and electricity.

(iii) The rural population moved from small scattered settlements to small towns which had proper sewage systems, water and power supplies.

(iv) Rural areas benefited from the expansion of council housing, especially after 1945, when many rural towns and villages were provided with cheaper rented housing by the local authorities.

Changes in Health in Rural and Urban Areas

Health in Urban Areas

Industrialisation led to the development of towns where people lived in overcrowded conditions. Poverty also contributed to a poor diet. This led to severe health problems in Britain's cities.

Changes Affecting Health

1880–1918

(i) Improvements in sanitation made under the 1875 Public Health Act led to a reduction in typhoid and cholera.

(ii) The main killer diseases were those caused by living in overcrowded, cold, damp living conditions: T.B., pneumonia and bronchitis. Infectious diseases like Scarlet Fever were also common in overcrowded conditions, where poor diet reduced resistance to disease.

(iii) Inadequate diet caused by poverty led to deficiency diseases such as rickets.

(iv) Standards of hygiene and nursing in hospitals had improved greatly by 1918. However, most hospitals charged fees. Charity hospitals which were open to the poor offered a much lower standard of care.

(v) The National Insurance Act 1911 provided free medical treatment for workers who had made sufficient contributions. Their wives and children were not covered.

1918–1939

Some of the worst effects of industrialisation on health were eased during this period.

(i) There was increased Government concern with standards of health. In 1919, the Ministry of Health was established, which organised campaigns to encourage a healthier life-style.

(ii) Improvements in housing had a positive effect on health.

(iii) Improvements in medicine, e.g. anti-biotics.

(iv) Those in work during this period saw a rise in their real wages and a general improvement in their living conditions.

However, health care remained expensive. Despite Government and voluntary health insurance schemes, adequate health care was beyond the reach of many of the lower paid.

1939–1990

The introduction of the National Health Service (NHS) in 1948 did most to tackle health problems during this period. Free health care was made available to all.

The main features of the National Health Service were:
  (i) Completely free care from doctors, dentists, opticians and hospitals.
 (ii) Regional Hospital Boards were set up by the Government to organise and run all hospitals.
(iii) Local Health Authorities were established to control maternity and child care, home nursing and ambulance services.
(iv) Executive Councils, made up of local citizens and representatives of the medical profession, were set up to supervise doctors, dentists, opticians and pharmacists.

Changes in the National Health Service

The cost to Government of providing these services rose dramatically as medical technology developed and people started living longer. Charges for health care were first introduced in 1951 and after 1979, the Government looked for ways of controlling Government spending on the N.H.S. and encouraging private health care.

Health in Rural Areas

Standards of health in rural areas generally improved during this period. Before 1914, school inspections revealed that children living in rural areas were generally heavier and taller than those living in the cities.

Reasons
  (i) After 1880, women and children worked less in open air in all weathers.
 (ii) There was a general improvement in wages and living conditions for agricultural workers.

(iii) The diet in rural areas tended to be better than in urban areas. There was better access to fresh food. More of the family budget was spent on food as there were fewer other things to buy in rural areas.

Impact of the National Health Service on Rural Areas

Although people in rural areas shared in most of the benefits of the new health service, the reorganisation of health care had some disadvantages. The closing or downgrading of local cottage hospitals meant that people had to travel to hospitals in the larger towns to receive treatment.

8

Changes in Employment and Working Conditions for Women

Industrial change in the period 1880–1990 contributed to an increase in the employment of women. There was some improvement in women's working conditions and some steps were made towards female equality in the workplace.

1880–1918

Women at Work before 1914

Employment

In 1881, 1·5 million women in Scotland worked compared to 2·1 million men. The most common source of employment for women was in domestic service. Legislation in the 1840s excluded women from heavy industries such as coal mining but many women worked in textile mills.

Working conditions

Women worked long hours for low pay. On average, they earned less than half what men earned. There were some changes in working conditions before 1914.

(i) Invention of the typewriter and telephone opened up work for women in offices. It was cheaper to employ women for office work.

(ii) The 1872 Education Act improved educational opportunities for girls, making it easier for them to get work in shops and offices. A few women managed to fight their way into the professions.

(iii) Some success was achieved in organising women factory workers into trade unions to improve working conditions.

      1888 — Match Girls' Strike

      1889 — Women Trade Unionists' League.

(iv) Government appointed women Factory Inspectors for the first time.

Effects of First World War on Employment and Working Conditions

Employment

The need to increase industrial and agricultural output forced the Government and other employers to take on more women workers.

Increase in numbers of women working 1914–1919:

Area of Employment	Increase in Number of Women Workers
Armed Forces	100 000
Nursing	100 000
Government	200 000
Farm work	250 000
Office work	500 000
Engineering (including munitions)	800 000

Working conditions

In many cases, women worked in unpleasant, dirty or dangerous conditions. However, those doing vital war work found that their pay increased. By the end of the war, the average weekly wage for a woman was £2.00. Before the war, the average was 58p.

1918–1939

Employment

1931 Census — Types of work done by women in Scotland.	
Domestic Service	138 679
Commercial Occupations, e.g. shop work	95 919
Textiles	81 668
Office Work	77 451
Professions	48 876

Working Conditions

  (i) Middle class women had more opportunities than before the war. The 1919 Sex Disqualification Act removed restrictions on women entering universities and the professions.

 (ii) Working class women, many of whom had done skilled work during the war, generally left these jobs to make way for men returning from the services. The slump of the inter-war years meant there were fewer semi-skilled or skilled jobs.

(iii) The development of 'new industries' created more openings for women on the new assembly lines or in offices.

(iv) The Marriage Bar — Legislation banned married women working in Government posts. Many private employers also operated a marriage bar.

1939–1990

The Second World War created a need for women workers to an even greater extent than in the First World War. Conscription for women was introduced and there was assistance to women through the provision of nurseries and the ending of restrictions on married women working.

Steps towards equality in the workplace since 1945

  (i) 1955 — Equal pay for women in the Civil Service.

 (ii) 1970 — Equal Pay Act made it illegal for a woman to be paid less than a man for doing the same work.

(iii) 1975 — Equal Opportunities Act made it illegal to discriminate against women when appointing someone for a job.

(iv) 1984 — Equal Pay Act ensured that women were entitled to the same pay as men doing work of equivalent value.

An Equal Opportunities Commission report in 1986 revealed that women were still doing less skilled, poorer paid jobs than men. The average wage of a woman was estimated to be 25% less than that of a man.

Women in the professions (1985):

Profession	Men	Women
Judges/Lawyers	45 000	8 000
Doctors	60 000	19 000
Accountants	204 000	23 000
Scientists/Engineers	896 000	87 000

9

The Role of Trade Unions in Changing Working Conditions

1880–1918

Trade union membership in Britain

    1880 — 0·5 million
    1888 — 0·75 million
    1900 — 2·0 million

Before 1880, trade union membership was mainly confined to skilled workers. The late 1880s and early 1890s saw a great increase in the membership of 'new unions' representing the semi-skilled and unskilled.

Reasons for the growth of new unions

(i) Low unemployment in the 1880s and early 1890s helped growth in membership. Unions found it easier to make progress when workers were in short supply and employers were more willing to negotiate with their workforce.

(ii) A series of successful strikes where unskilled workers obtained better conditions encouraged other unskilled workers to join unions.

1888 — Match-girls' strike
One thousand four hundred girls from Bryant and May's factory, whose wages were as low as 20p a week and who faced severe health risks due to working with phosphorous, organised a successful strike for improved conditions.

1889 — Dock strike
London dockers suffered irregular employment and earned only 2p an hour. Their strike was successful in gaining a small pay increase and a guaranteed minimum of four hours work.

(iii) Socialist agitators assisted workers in organising themselves and conducting strikes. In the match-girls' strike, the socialist writer Annie Besant helped to publicise the workers' cause and helped to organise the strike. The dockers' strike was led by socialists Ben Tillet and Tom Mann.

Between 1900 and 1914, disputes became increasingly bitter. Employers fought back by organising lock-outs. The Government intervened to help employers break strikes using police and army.

During the war years, trade unions generally cooperated with the war effort and the number of strikes decreased.

1918–1939

During the inter-war period, trade unions had little success in improving the working conditions of their members.

Reasons

(i) The 1920s slump and the depression of the 1930s brought high unemployment. During these times, employers were less willing to improve conditions for their workers and could replace workers who were union activists.

(ii) Fall in trade union membership
   1920 — 8 million
   1926 — 5 million
   1933 — 4 million

(iii) A series of unsuccessful strikes culminated in the disastrous General Strike of 1926, when 1·5 million workers were called out on strike in support of the miners' claim for better pay and conditions. The strike collapsed within ten days.

1939–1990

British Trade Union Membership 1938–1988
   1938 — 6 003 000
   1948 — 9 632 000
   1958 — 9 639 000
   1968 — 10 049 000
   1978 — 12 173 000
   1988 — 8 003 000

Trade Unions in the Second World War

Trade unions again co-operated closely with Government in the war effort and were able to obtain substantial improvements in the working conditions of people engaged in war work. Some trade union leaders were able to gain important positions in Government, e.g. Ernest Bevin of the transport workers was given a place in the war cabinet.

Rise and Fall of Union Power 1945–1990

The strength of trade unions increased during the prosperous years of the 1950s, 1960s and early 1970s. Unions played a major role in bringing an improvement in wages and conditions during this period.

Union leaders rejected the attempts of the Labour Government to bring about pay restraint in 1969 and 1977. The miners' union succeeded in bringing down the Conservative Government of Edward Heath in 1974.

After 1980, however, the power of the unions to influence employment and conditions was reduced.

Reasons

(i) High unemployment meant that unions lost members. Workers were more reluctant to strike for fear of losing their jobs.

(ii) The Conservatives introduced anti-union legislation, e.g. strike calls must be supported by 80% of the workforce.

(iii) Unsuccessful strike action during this period, most notably the failure of the 1984–1985 miners' strike.

By the end of the 1980s, trade unions had less power to win improvements in working conditions for their members by negotiation or industrial action. Many unions have gone back to doing what the original 19th century 'craft unions' did, i.e. arranging insurance schemes and other benefits for their members.

10

Parliamentary Reform in Scotland and England After 1884

The Extension of the Franchise in the 20th Century

(i) 1918 — Representation of the People Act. This extended the franchise by giving the vote to:
  (a) all men over 21,
  (b) all women over 30.

(ii) 1928 Act — This gave the vote to all women on the same basis as men.

(iii) 1969 Act — The voting age was lowered from 21 to 18.

The Movement for Women's Suffrage, 1980s–1928 (see 1830s–1930s).

UNIT 2 — International Co-operation and Conflict

CONTEXT B: 1890s–1920s

PART ONE — 1890–1914

1

The Great Powers and their Alliances, 1894–1914

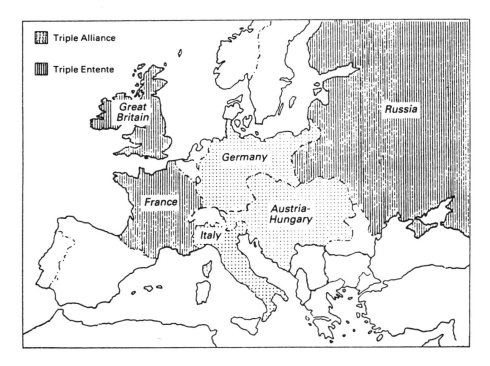

Background

1. In *Germany*, *Kaiser Wilhelm II* took over in 1890. He wanted Germany to be a great country with colonies ('a place in the sun'), a navy and close alliances. He upset the stability of Europe by his aggressive attitude.

2. In *France* there was anger at the loss of Alsace and Lorraine to Germany during the 1870–1871 war. There was a strong feeling amongst the French for revenge and to regain the lost land. France was also keen to increase her overseas Empire.

3. In *Austria-Hungary* there were many different nationalities, e.g. Croats and Serbs. The old Emperor, Franz Joseph, had difficulty in controlling the nationalist aspirations of these racial groups who wanted their independence.

4. *Russia* was the largest country in the world but was also industrially very backward. As a result, her large army, sometimes called 'the Russian steamroller', was in fact very weak as it did not have modern weapons.

5. *Britain*, as an island, depended on her navy for security. Although she had a very small army (approximately 90 000), she had the potential of increasing it through the support of the countries in her world-wide Empire, e.g. Australia, New Zealand, Canada and India.

Alliance System — By 1914, Europe was divided into two armed camps.

1. The Central Powers formed the *Triple Alliance*.

| 1879 | Dual Alliance | Germany and Austria-Hungary |
| 1882 | Triple Alliance | Italy joined Germany and Austria-Hungary |

These alliances had been formed by Chancellor Bismarck of Germany who wanted to preserve peace by isolating France.

2. The Allied Powers formed the *Triple Entente*.

In 1892, France and Russia formed a Dual Alliance. This was a military agreement made to protect each other from attack by Germany alone or attack from all the Triple Alliance countries. If either France or Russia was attacked, the other would come to its aid.

Britain was therefore isolated from these alliances and stood in *splendid isolation*. In 1902, she came out of isolation and made an agreement in the Far East with Japan. As Britain became more concerned about German ambitions and its desire to build a large navy, she made moves to befriend European powers. In 1904, she formed the *Entente Cordiale* with France.

Having made friends with France, it was only natural that she should also befriend France's alliance partner, Russia. In 1907 this happened.

| 1904 | Entente Cordiale | Britain and France | Settled colonial differences over Morocco and Egypt |
| 1907 | Triple Entente | Russia joined with Britain and France | Britain settled differences with Russia over Persia and Afghanistan |

N.B. There was an important difference between the 'Triple Alliance' and the Triple Entente:

Triple Alliance — firm agreement to come to the aid of the attacked country — Germany, Austria-Hungary, Italy.

Triple Entente — a friendly agreement settling colonial differences with no commitment to come to each other's aid, i.e. not a military alliance — Britain, France, Russia.

It should be noted that by 1914, Britain and France had become closer allies with the signing, in 1911, of a secret naval agreement between the countries — the British navy would patrol the Atlantic while the French navy would patrol the Mediterranean. This made Britain more *morally obligated* to come to the aid of France if attacked.

Summary

By 1914, Europe was divided into two armed camps — the Triple Alliance and the Triple Entente. This alliance system made countries behave more boldly than before since they had allies to help them.

2

International Tension as shown in

1. The Naval Arms Race

In 1898, the Kaiser decided that Germany needed a larger navy. Britain viewed this as a direct challenge to her control of the seas. In 1906, Britain introduced a new type of battleship, the *Dreadnought*.

The main advantages of the *Dreadnought* over previous battleships were:
  (i) armour plating was thicker,
 (ii) guns had a greater range,
(iii) faster.

The new dreadnoughts made all earlier battleships obsolete (out of date). This new technology worked to Germany's advantage as she only had a small navy and could race Britain to build the biggest number of dreadnoughts.

Britain won the race to build dreadnoughts, with Britain building 29 to Germany's 17 between 1906 and 1914. For Britain, control of the seas was vital as an island dependent on foreign trade, particularly food. Britain viewed the Kaiser's decision to build a navy as a direct threat and this contributed to the growing tension between Britain and Germany in the years leading up to World War One.

2. The Balkans 1908–1913

The Balkan problem stemmed from the following:
  (i) Turkey controlled much of the area but was very weak and in decline. The Turkish Empire was 'the sick man of Europe'.
 (ii) The Balkan people wanted rid of the Turks as Slav nationalism began to build up with the various Balkan nationalities wanting their independence.
(iii) Serbia already had independence and was anxious to acquire more land on the coast.
(iv) The major European powers of Russia, Austria-Hungary, Germany, and even Italy had an interest in the future of the Balkans.
  (a) Russia wanted all year round access to the Mediterranean through the Dardanelles and also viewed herself as protector of her fellow Slavs in the Balkans.

(b) Austria-Hungary contained Slavs and was anxious at Serbia's growing power and desire to increase her influence.

(c) Germany wanted to build a railway line from Berlin to Baghdad which would go through the Balkans.

(d) Italy wanted to gain additional land.

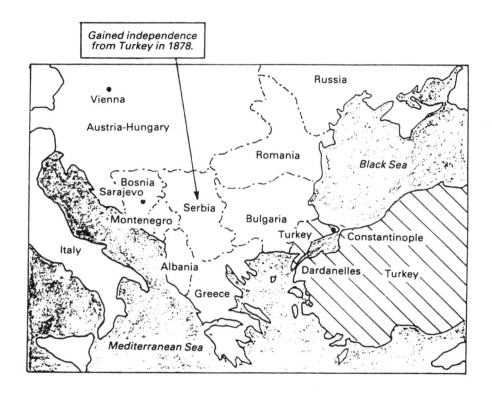

Gained independence from Turkey in 1878.

Crisis One — *Annexation of Bosnia-Herzegovina, 1908*

Austria-Hungary annexed (took over) Bosnia and Herzegovina, much to the anger of Serbia and the Serbs within Bosnia, who would have preferred to have joined Serbia. On this occasion, Serbia felt unable to take any action since Russia was not in a position to give any military support.

Crisis Two — *The Balkan Wars of 1912 and 1913*

By these wars the Turks were driven out of the Balkans. In the first Balkan War of 1912, the kingdoms of Greece, Bulgaria, Serbia and Montenegro combined together to defeat Turkey. By the Treaty of London, the Turks gave up all their land in the Balkans and this, after a new country *Albania* was created, was shared amongst the victors. The creation of Albania was at the insistence of Austria-Hungary and this angered Serbia, as she had wanted that coastal land for herself.

The victors of the first Balkan war squabbled over the spoils, and *Bulgaria* declared war on Greece and and Serbia. Turkey and Romania joined with Serbia and Greece to defeat Bulgaria. *Serbia* had, for the second time, been victorious in war with the result that

(i) Serbia had doubled in size.

(ii) The Serbs living in Bosnia and Herzegovina were more anxious to break away from Austria-Hungary and join Serbia.

(iii) Serbian nationalism was stronger than ever.

Crisis Three — *Sarajevo and the Outbreak of War*

Sarajevo was the capital of Bosnia. On June 28th, 1914, the heir to the Austro-Hungarian throne, Archduke Franz Ferdinand, and his wife, the Countess Sophie, were on an official visit. Gavrilo Princip, a 19-year-old student, shot both the Archduke and his wife. Austria blamed Serbia for the assassination for the following reasons:

(i) The assassination was planned in Belgrade (the capital of Serbia).

(ii) The weapons used by Princip and his fellow conspirators were provided by Serbian officers and had been given passage out of Serbia into Bosnia.

The assassination had been planned by the Black Hand Society which was a Serbian terrorist organisation. It was led by Colonel Apis, who was in the Serbian army. The aim of the Black Hand Society was to create a single Slav country out of the Balkans. Austria-Hungary took advantage of the situation to finish Serbia for once and for all. An *ultimatum* was sent to Serbia which

(i) made ten demands which virtually amounted to loss of independence,

(ii) gave her only 48 hours to agree to it,

(iii) if it was not accepted war would be declared.

Serbia accepted eight out of the ten demands and offered to put the remaining two to an international conference. This was not sufficient to satisfy Austria, and war was declared on Serbia on 28th July 1914.

The Outbreak of War

As a result of the *alliance system*, what started off as a *local* war escalated into a *world* war very quickly. The sequence of events was as follows:

28th June	— Archduke Franz Ferdinand, heir to the Austro-Hungarian throne, was assassinated.
5th July	— Germany agreed to support Austria and urged Austria to act without delay.
23rd July	— Austria-Hungary sent a harsh ultimatum to Serbia with a 48-hour time limit.
25th July	— Serbia accepted eight out of the ten points and was prepared to place the other two before an international conference.
28th July	— Austria-Hungary declared war on Serbia.
30th July	— Russia responded to Serbia's request for military assistance by ordering the mobilisation of her troops.
31st July	— Germany sent an ultimatum to Russia demanding a stop to her war preparations. If Russia would not demobilise then Germany would go to war against Russia.
1st August	— Tsar Nicholas II of Russia refused to demobilise and, as a result, Germany declared war on Russia. France, an ally of Russia, ordered the mobilisation of her troops.
3rd August	— Germany declared war on France. Germany invaded Belgium which was a neutral country. Britain sent an ultimatum to Germany to withdraw from Belgium since Britain had signed the 1839 Treaty of London which had guaranteed Belgium independence.
4th August	— Germany failed to respond to this British ultimatum with the result that Britain was at war with Germany.

With the exception of Italy, the five other powers which made up the Triple Entente and the Triple Alliance were at war.

Responsibility for World War One

The attitude and actions of all of the major powers, Austria-Hungary, Germany, Russia, France and Britain, contributed to the outbreak of World

War One. In particular the *alliance system* made countries *interdependent* on each other with Germany, for example, quickly coming to the aid of Austria-Hungary. Countries also behaved more aggressively in the knowledge that they had an ally to support them. In addition, these major countries had been preparing for war by building up their armies and navies and were, therefore, in a position to go to war.

In assessing war guilt, the following points should be considered.

	Against	*In defence of her actions*
Austria-Hungary	(i) ultimatum to Serbia was designed to provoke war	(i) assassination of the Archduke was planned in Serbia
	(ii) the Serbian reply should have been accepted by her	(ii) anticipated a local war and not one in which Russia would interfere.
Germany	(i) failed to restrain Austria-Hungary	(i) felt threatened by the Franco-Russian alliance
	(ii) escalated the war by declarations against Russia and France	(ii) to carry out a successful war on two fronts had to go through Belgium.
	(iii) violated Belgian neutrality.	
Russia	(i) mobilised quickly to respond to Serbia's call for assistance. This action immediately escalated the war beyond that of a local war.	(i) Russia had stood back in 1908 and allowed Austria-Hungary to annex Bosnia and Herzegovina. She could not allow Austria to expand further.
		(ii) She viewed herself as protector of the Slavs.
France	(i) failed to restrain her ally, Russia	(i) was brought into the war by Germany's declaration of war.
Britain	(i) failed to restrain her entente partner, Russia	(i) Britain had signed the Treaty of London, 1839, which had guaranteed Belgian neutrality and felt compelled to stand by it.
	(ii) failed to make clear to Germany that she was prepared to go to war over Belgium until it was too late.	

At the end of World War One the victorious allies accused Germany of having caused the war (War Guilt Clause 231) and this caused much resentment within Germany. It also led to the allies imposing heavy reparations on Germany.

Summary

International tension had been created in the decade leading up to World War One by the attitudes and actions of the major powers as the diagram below illustrates.

Britain and Germany
Britain was suspicious of Germany's motives in building up a navy.

France and Germany
French desire to regain the lost land of Alsace and Lorraine from Germany.

International
Tension
1900–1914

Austria-Hungary and Russia
Anxiety by both powers as to what should happen to the unsettled Balkan area — they held opposite views.

Austria-Hungary and Serbia
Serbia's desire to expand and form a large independent Slav state worried Austria-Hungary, who had many Slavs in her empire and did not want her empire to break up.

PART 2 — 1914–1918

3

The Experience of War, 1914–1918, and its Effects on the Lives of Civilians in Britain.

(i) *Recruitment*

   (a) At the outbreak of the war, Britain had a small professional army of 90 000 men. Immediately Lord Kitchener introduced a recruitment campaign which asked for volunteers and was an immediate success. By the end of 1915, however, the high casualty rate and drop in volunteers forced the government to reluctantly change its policy.

   (b) *Conscription* was introduced in January, 1916, for single men aged 18–41. In June this was extended to married men.

   Tribunals were set up to listen to claims from *conscientious objectors* as to why they should be exempted from joining the armed services. Many of the 16 000 conscientious objectors were from religious groups like Quakers or Jehovah's Witnesses who were opposed to fighting. Some "conchies" accepted non-combat duties, like stretcher bearers, but there was a hard core of 1500 objectors who refused to have anything to do with the war. These people were called *absolutists* and were sent to prison, where they were treated very harshly.

(ii) *Propaganda* was used by the Government by

   (a) portraying the Germans as murderers of women and children in their invasion of Belgium;

   (b) distributing recruitment posters to encourage men to volunteer for the army;

   (c) censoring and selecting items of news relating to the war so that morale would remain high.

(iii) *Employment*

   (a) An opportunity presented itself for *women* as a result of the large number of men volunteering to join the army. With the introduction of conscription in 1916, the need for women to take the work from men became even more necessary. They took employment in areas directly related to the war — nurses, doctors, munition workers and the women's branches of the armed forces (WAAC and WRENS). They also took employment in other areas — farming, shipbuilding, trams, buses, railways, civil service.

(b) Some men were exempted from conscription to the army because they were in reserved occupations (occupations needed for the war), e.g. shipbuilding and coal mining.

(iv) *Food Supplies*

Britain depended on her merchant navy bringing in her food from abroad. When the war broke out in 1914, 100% of all sugar, 65% of all butter and 40% of all meat came from overseas.

Food shortages became a problem in 1917, when Germany introduced a policy of *unrestricted submarine warfare*. By using submarines to sink British merchant ships, Germany hoped to starve Britain into submission. By April 1917, Britain only had six weeks supply of food left. The food shortage problem was tackled in four ways by

(1) *propaganda posters* urging people not to waste food;

(2) *increasing food production* within Britain by bringing more land, including town allotments, under cultivation;

(3) *rationing* some items of food by introducing ration cards which ensured a fair distribution of food. In 1918, sugar, meat, butter and tea were all rationed. Items which contained sugar, such as jam and marmalade, were also rationed.

(4) introducing the *convoy system* to reduce the number of merchant ships being sunk.

(v) *Government Control*

(a) The Liberal Government got Parliament to pass a *Defence of the Realm Act* (DORA) in 1914, so that emergency measures could be taken. Through this act, the Government introduced a variety of war-time measures which included

(1) *Censorship* of war news in the papers;

(2) arrest of *aliens* (foreign citizens);

(3) restrictions in *licensing hours* to cut down drunkenness and absenteeism from work;

(4) Restrictions in *street lighting*;

(5) Food *rationing*.

(b) The government took control of the *industries* vital to conducting the war, e.g. mines, agriculture, railways.

In May 1915, Asquith formed a *Coalition Government* from all three political parties. In November 1916, Asquith was replaced as Prime Minister by the energetic Minister of Munitions, Lloyd George.

(vi) *Civilians at Risk*

In comparison to World War Two, very few civilians lived in fear of bombing attacks from the air. However, civilians were affected by

(a) Aerial attacks from *zeppelins* at the beginning of the war, and *Gotha bombers* at the end of the war.

(b) Sea attack on Scarborough, Hartlepool and Whitby in 1914.

Bombing of civilian targets resulted in the deaths of 1414 people in England. Although limited, it did have a demoralising effect on the population.

(vii) *Cost of the War*

The war was costly both in *human* and *financial* terms. In total, over eight million soldiers were killed during the war of whom 0·75 million came from Britain and her Empire. One out of every five British soldiers died during the war, and hardly a family in Britain would not have been affected by the death of some relative or friend.

In addition to these figures, there were many soldiers who came back from the war seriously wounded, some blinded, some deaf, some crippled for life. Almost 20 million men were wounded during the war, of whom 1·5 million came from Britain and her Empire. This amounted to one in every two returning British soldiers coming back from the war wounded.

Reasons for the High Loss of Human Life

(a) New technology of warfare, in particular the machine gun and heavy artillery.

(b) Nature of trench warfare.

(c) War of attrition.

(d) 'Total war', with industry controlled by Government to produce more weapons and shells.

(e) Poor leadership.

(f) Medical assistance delayed.

(f) A lengthy war involving many countries.

The *financial* cost of the war was also great and countries had to borrow heavily. For Britain, the cost of the war was £7·9 million and emerged from the war heavily in debt.

(viii) *Change in attitude towards war*

When World War One broke out in 1914, there was almost an enthusiasm for war throughout Europe. In Britain, for example, men rushed to volunteer for service because

(a) they were caught up in the war fever and the 'need to do their bit for King and Country';

(b) they believed the war would be short and over by Christmas;

(c) they were attracted by the excitement of going abroad;

(d) they had a false impression of the nature of warfare being glorious with hand-to-hand combat.

By 1916, a change in attitude to war was very evident as the war dragged on and the number of casualties increased. Civilians also began to suffer through food shortages and, with conscription, very few families were to be unaffected by the war. The death of a close member of the family destroyed the myth of a glorious war.

Come the end of the war, the attitude to war had changed completely and there was considerable rejoicing when an armistice was signed with Germany to take effect from 11th November, 1918.

(ix) *Change in attitude towards women*

(a) At the outbreak of war, the suffragettes abandoned their campaign for the vote and gave full support to the war. By the end of the war, attitudes to women receiving the vote had changed due to their contribution to the war effort. As a result, in 1918 women aged 30 or more received the vote.

(b) The place of women in the workforce changed as a result of women taking the jobs of men.

(c) It became more acceptable for women to go out unchaperoned, wear cosmetics, smoke and drink in public places.

(d) Attitudes towards sex became more liberal and by the end of the war the illegitimacy rate had increased by 30%.

4

The Experience of War, 1914–1918, and its Effects on People's Lives in Germany.

(i) *Recruitment*

At the outbreak of war, Germany already had conscription and a standing army of 856 000 which could be augmented by 3 800 000 trained reserves.

(ii) *Propaganda*

Germany used similar propaganda techniques as Britain. There were similar atrocity stories as appeared in the British press. One of the most successful was the report that the French had tried to infect a well at Metz with cholera bacilli. Other reports had German prisoners having their eyes gouged out.

(iii) *Employment*

As the war progressed, Germany had difficulty in replacing the loss of skilled workers. As in Britain, the war provided an opportunity for women to take on new jobs.

(iv) *Food Supplies*

Germany imported one-third of her food and suffered serious food shortages as a result of Britain's naval blockade. As a result, Germany tackled the problem by

(1) increasing food production where possible. This included growing food in public parks;

(2) introducing in 1917 an elaborate system of rationing which included bread, milk, butter, meat, fats and clothes;

(3) introducing *substitute foods* such as clover meal and chestnut flour.

Despite these measures, Germany suffered very much more than Britain. Men had to live on a ration which gave them only half the calories needed by manual workers. Meat consumption was down to a quarter of what it had been in 1914. As a result of this shortage of food, Germans were more vulnerable to the flu epidemic which hit Europe at the end of the war and almost a million died.

(v) *Government Control*

In Germany, industry was more systematically controlled than in Britain. This was due to the work of the industrialist Walter Rathenau, who brought the main industries under government control. By the end of the war, German industry was suffering from the naval blockade and there were shortages of essential war materials such as fuel and chemicals.

(vi) *Civilians at Risk*

It was not until 1918 that British air raids took place over Germany and the Rhineland. These raids led to a loss of morale amongst the civilian population.

(vii) *Cost of the War*

For Germany, the cost of the war was greater than any other country. Up until the end of 1917, Germany was fighting a war on two fronts (the western front in France and the eastern front in Russia) and the number of deaths totalled two million. An additional 4·25 million Germans were wounded.

The financial cost of the war totalled £8·4 million and placed an enormous burden on the government and the German people.

(viii) *Change in Attitude Towards War*

At first the German people had welcomed the war but by 1918 that attitude had changed. There were several reasons for this:

(a) America's entry into the war in 1917 was psychologically very damaging. Many Germans believed that victory was no longer possible due to America's unlimited economic power and military potential.

(b) The impact of the British naval blockade.

(c) The failure of the 1918 spring offensives which were costly in human lives.

5

New Technology and its Effects on the Conduct of War on the Western Front, 1914–1918.

Trench Warfare

The opening months of the war, in 1914, was a war of movement, with the German army attempting to carry out the Schlieffen plan and defeat France within six weeks. When the Germans were halted at the battle of the Marne and then failed to capture the Channel ports at the first battle of Ypres, they dug a line of trenches to hold the land they had gained.

As the map below shows the line of trenches stretched from the Belgian coast, across the north of France, to Switzerland.

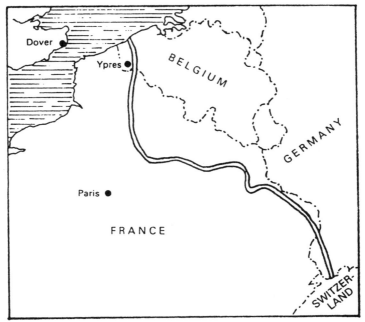

The Line of the Trenches, early 1915.

Both sides dug trenches which had the following features

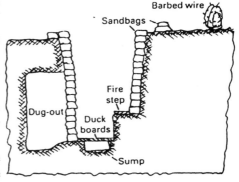

- (i) the trenches were *zig-zagged* to reduce the impact of fire power;
- (ii) trenches were about *2 metres* in depth;
- (iii) wooden slats formed a *duck-board* for walking on;
- (iv) a *drainage sump* below the duck-board was designed to take away the water;
- (v) a *firestep* allowed soldiers to be able to fire over the top of the trench with their rifles;

(vi) *sand bags* were used as parapets at the top of the trench to provide additional protection;

(vii) *barbed wire* was placed in front of the trench to slow down the enemy as they approached and make them easy targets;

(viii) *dugouts* for men to sleep in and supplies to be kept.

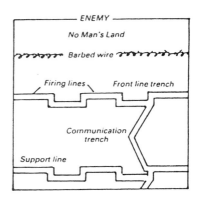

The trench system was built up of front line trenches, communication trenches and support line trenches. The area between the opposing sides' front line trenches was called *No Man's Land*.

The Effect of Trench Warfare on the Conduct of the War

Trench warfare resulted in

(i) a *high number of casualties*, since there was so little protection for troops who went into attack;

(ii) a war of *attrition* developing where battles would last for several months as each side tried to wear the other down;

(iii) *hard conditions* for the ordinary soldier;

(iv) a *protracted war* where it would take a long time for any side to overcome the other side's defences to such an extent that the war would end.

New Technology and its Effects on the Conduct of War on the Western Front, 1914–1918

As the war progressed so did the technology and killing power of the weapons. The *cavalry* was not to play a significant part in this war, although horses had a role to play in transportation.

Weapons and their use	Effect on the Conduct of the War
Heavy artillery — howitzers were used in the artillery bombardments which preceded an attack. At the Somme, for example, Britain used 1500 guns and fired 1·5 million shells in seven days. The purpose of these bombardments was to destroy enemy trenches, dugouts, barbed wire and artillery.	1. Caused more casualties than any other weapon in the war. 2. Little protection for the soldiers although steel helmets were issued and dugouts made deeper. 3. Destroyed enemy trenches and created large crater holes in No Man's Land. 4. Failed to destroy the barbed wire which was simply thrown up into the air only to drop down again intact. 5. Made obvious where an attack was about to begin because aircraft could spot the artillery moving into place.
Machine guns were able to fire in the region of 500 rounds a minute. At first Britain did not appreciate as much as the Germans the full value of this weapon, but with trench warfare, its rapid fire power was evident to the British generals as being vital in defending a trench from enemy attack.	1. Next to the heavy artillery accounted for most casualties. 2. The tank was developed to help overcome the problems brought about by the machine gun's rapid fire.
The *tank's* main features were caterpillar tracks to get over rough land, armour plating to overcome the machine gun fire, and a fascine to get over trenches. 'Male' tanks were fitted with field guns, 'female' tanks were fitted with machine guns. They were slow moving and better suited to dry conditions, used in large numbers, with plenty of support troops to consolidate the land gained.	1. Invented by the British, they made their first appearance at the Somme in 1916. Unfortunately, many broke down and the element of surprise was lost. 2. Improvements in the tank led to a successful breakthough by 378 tanks on the chalky soil at Cambrai (1917), but there were insufficient support troops to hold the land gained. 3. In 1918, the tank was again used in large numbers and without an artillery bombardment sent the Germans into retreat.
Gas shells came in two types — *chlorine gas*, which caused choking, and *mustard gas*, which caused burns. Mustard gas was a lot worse since it was invisible and caused blindness. The effectiveness of gas as a weapon was restricted by the possibility of changing winds and the development of gas masks.	1. Chlorine gas was used by the Germans for the first time at the second battle of Ypres (1915). While it caught the British and French by surprise, the Germans had insufficient troops to capitalise on the breakthrough. 2. Mustard gas was used for the first time, in 1917, by the Germans. The British gas mask provided no protection against it. 3. After 1917, the Germans ran out of chemicals and gas was rarely used. Overall, gas attacks caused few deaths, but were responsible for many soldiers losing their sight.

Weapons and their use	Effect on the Conduct of the War
Aeroplanes were in their infancy when war broke out, but German airships, *zeppelins*, carried out raids on England. By the end of the war, aeroplane technology had improved to such an extent that German Gotha bombers could attack Britain from Belgium. In the main, planes were used for reconnaissance (observation) on the Western Front.	1. Aeroplanes had little effect on the conduct of the war. Few civilians were killed from either the zeppelin or other air raids.

6

The Experience of War, 1914–1918, and its Effects on the Lives of Soldiers on the Western Front.

(i) *Military discipline*

Civilians had very quickly to adjust to the rigours of obeying orders without question and following the strict military discipline. Soldiers found guilty of cowardice, sleeping while on sentry duty, deserting or failing to obey orders were court-martialled and given the death sentence.

(ii) *Psychological Damage*

New recruits had to overcome the unnerving sight of seeing graveyards and hearing the sound of heavy gunfire. The experience of killing the enemy at close range for the first time was one soldiers rarely forgot.

(iii) *Constant Fear of Death*

For those soldiers in the front line each day brought the possibility of death. Enemy snipers were always on the look out for a target and, during the afternoon strafe between 2 p.m. and 4 p.m., German minnies were fired into British trenches. At night time, when soldiers were sent out to repair the parapets or barbed wire, a flare might illuminate the sky and the soldiers would become easy targets.

An attack was always costly in human lives. The preliminary artillery bombardment resulted in many soldiers being buried alive. 'Going over the top' into the unprotected No Man's Land amidst exploding shells, rapid machine gun fire and rifle fire always brought a high number of casualties. For example, at the Battle of the Somme in July 1916, Britain suffered 60 000 casualties (20 000 dead) on the first day. By the end of the battle in November, British losses totalled 420 000.

(iv) *Treatment for the Wounded*

There were no drugs like penicillin or X-rays to help doctors treat the injured. Nontheless, the Royal Army Medical Corps developed a well organised system to deal with the wounded. Each battalion had 16 stretcher bearers which was doubled to 32 before an attack. The wounded were taken back to a support trench where dressings would be applied and only the most urgent cases operated on. From these aid posts, the wounded were moved back to the main dressing stations where some emergency operations took place when necessary. The wounded were then taken back to casualty clearing stations where about 1000 soldiers could be treated. Only those who needed a lengthier time to recover were sent back to Britain. This well organised system was superior to the French and had better supplies than the Germans. About 80% of those who passed through this system eventually returned to some form of duty.

(v) *Dull Daily Routine*

Day to day life in the trenches was dull and spent by:

(a) cleaning weapons,
(b) filling sandbags,
(c) digging/repairing trenches,
(d) reading/writing letters (which might be censored),
(e) having a medical check up for lice, trench foot or other ailments.

(vi) *Wretched Living Conditions*

(a) troops slept in dug-outs which gave little protection (only slept about four hours a night),
(b) smell of death from decaying bodies,
(c) open latrines,
(d) exposed to rain, mud and frost,
(e) monotonous food of bully beef, bread and jam,
(f) shortage of drinking water,
(g) rats and lice.

(vii) *Changing Attitude to War*

In 1914, civilians were 'enthusiastic' to join the war and show their 'patriotism'. By 1917, many soldiers were 'disillusioned' (fed up) and had nothing but contempt for the commanding officers.

The Treaty of Versailles, 1919, and the Treatment of Germany

Germany Seeks an Armistice

During the war, the influence of the Kaiser, Wilhelm II, declined within Germany as the army high command of Hindenburg and Ludendorff indirectly ruled Germany. In 1918, the Kaiser was advised that the best course of action would be for him to *abdicate* and seek *safety* in neutral Holland. By this time, Germany's position was hopeless because

  (i) her allies, Austria, Hungary, Bulgaria and Turkey, were collapsing;

 (ii) her military position on the Western Front was hopeless, following the arrival of American troops and the Allied counter-offensives which had the Germans in retreat;

(iii) the German fleet mutinied;

(iv) within Germany, the conditions had become so bad that there were uprisings throughout the country;

 (v) the German High Command believed that if the Kaiser abdicated and Germany became a democratic republic, then better peace terms could be negotiated.

The Kaiser abdicated and fled to Holland. Two days later, on 11th November 1918, Germany agreed to an armistice and fighting was to cease as from 11 a.m.

The Peacemakers

In January 1919, over 30 countries met at the Palace of Versailles in Paris. Three men dominated this conference as a result of the status and influence of their countries.

 (i) *Prime Minister Clemenceau of France*

Georges Clemenceau was 70 years old when the war ended and had twice seen his country invaded by Germany. He had rejected suggestions for a compromise peace during the war, and was determined that France should now get her revenge for the huge losses suffered during the war.

Within France, Clemenceau stood in high esteem at the end of the war.

Expectations within France were high that, through Clemenceau, France would achieve her peace aims at Versailles. Her aims were:

(a) to make Germany pay for the damage caused to France through huge *reparations*;

(b) to make Germany return *Alsace and Lorraine* to France;

(c) to disarm Germany;

(d) to make Germany lose as much land as possible so that France would dominate Europe.

(e) to guarantee French security by Germany losing the Rhineland.

Clemenceau, nicknamed the Old Tiger, was successful in achieving his first three aims, but failed in the other two. Within France there was disappointment with the terms of Versailles.

(ii) *President Wilson of the USA*

When war broke out, the United States remained neutral. Despite the sinking of the *Lusitania* in 1915, with the loss of 128 American lives, the American Democrat President, Woodrow Wilson, fought the 1916 election partly on how he had kept America out of the war. Eventually, in 1917, America declared war after American ships had been sunk by German submarines. By the end of the war, only four American divisions had arrived in France. Not surprisingly, American lives lost totalled only 100 000 with a further 200 000 wounded.

Before the war ended, Woodrow Wilson produced his 'Fourteen Points' upon which he hoped the peace settlement would be made. Wilson drew up these points in January 1918, at a time when America had hardly suffered from the war. He was an 'idealist' who believed that:

(a) *national self-determination*, i.e. a nation's right to its own country and government, should be the guiding principle of the treaty;

(b) an international organisation, a *League of Nations*, should be set up to prevent future wars;

(c) all countries should *disarm* and there should be no more secret agreements between countries.

Germany's Reaction to the Fourteen Points

Germany favoured the proposals of Wilson as a basis for a peace settlement, because her loss of land would be limited to that of Alsace-

Lorraine, possibly colonies, and possibly land to give Poland access to the sea. There was no mention of 'war guilt' or having to pay 'reparations'.

France's Reaction to the Fourteen Points

Clemenceau was prepared to accept Wilson's principle of 'national self-determination' for redrawing the map of Europe. However, he wanted Germany punished and French security established. Clemenceau, therefore, was wanting a punitive settlement on Germany and was not in agreement with Wilson.

Wilson was a major influence at Versailles but his influence within America was insufficient to persuade the Senate to join the League of Nations after the war.

(iii) *Lloyd George, Prime Minister of Britain*

Lloyd George had won the 1918 election on slogans such as 'hang the Kaiser' and 'squeeze the German lemon until the pips squeak'. However, he was not as anti-German as Clemenceau and stood as a moderating force between Clemenceau and Wilson. He wanted:

(a) Britain's security to be gained by the destruction of the German fleet and airforce;

(b) Britain's trading with Germany to remain strong by preventing Germany being economically destroyed;

(c) to avoid France dominating Europe and was anxious that plebiscites be held to decide what land Germany should lose.

Terms of the Treaty of Versailles

1. Alsace and Lorraine
2. Eupen and Malmedy
3. Northern Schleswig
4. West Prussia
5. Danzig
6. Posen
7. Upper Silesia
8. Saar Coalfields

A   *Loss of Land by Germany*

    (i) Alsace and Lorraine restored to France.

    (ii) Eupen and Malmedy given to Belgium.

    (iii) Northern Schleswig returned to Denmark after a plebiscite.

    (iv) *(a)* West Prussia given to Poland in order to give Poland access to the sea. The port of Danzig to be a free city administered by the League of Nations because 100% of the population was German.

        (b) Posen given to Poland.

        (c) Part of Upper Silesia given to Poland after a plebiscite.

    (v) All her colonies.

As a result of these terms Germany lost 13% of its area, 12% of its population, 16% of its coal resources and 48% of its iron production.

B   *Disarmament of Germany*

    (i) Army limited to 100 000.

    (ii) No tanks, airforce or submarines allowed.

    (iii) Navy limited to six light battleships.

    (iv) No German troops or defences allowed in the Rhineland.

C   *Other terms on Germany*

    (i) By the War Guilt Clause (231), Germany was held responsible for starting the war and would have to pay *reparations* (damages). The figure for reparations was fixed at £6600 million in 1922.

    (ii) An army of occupation was to remain in the Ruhr for 15 years.

    (iii) Germany was not allowed to join with Austria.

    (iv) The Saar coalfields were given to France for 15 years.

German Response to the Treaty

On 28th June 1919, the German delegates signed the treaty because they had no choice. Had the Germans not signed then the allies would have restarted the war. Nonetheless, the Germans were very angry about

    (i) the fact that it was a *diktat* and the Germans were not allowed to be part of the conference;

    (ii) the *War Guilt Clause*, since other countries had responsibility in bringing about the war;

(iii) the extent of the *loss of land to Poland*;

(iv) the level of *reparations*, particularly since the loss of land and colonies appeared to take away Germany's means of paying them.

In comparison to the terms Germany imposed on Russia at Brest-Litovsk (see page 102), Germany, arguably, had little to complain about.

8

The Search for Security Through the League of Nations, 1919–1928

As part of the treaties of 1919, it was agreed to develop Woodrow Wilson's fourteenth point and set up an international organisation to provide security for all countries.

The League had three main *aims*.

(i) To maintain peace through all member countries agreeing to come to the aid of another member if attacked — this was called *collective* security.

(ii) To bring about *disarmament*.

(iii) To *improve social conditions* throughout the world.

The League was organised into different bodies.

(i) The *Council* — a small body of eight powers which would meet if a crisis arose. It was made up of four permanent major powers — Britain, France, Japan and Italy — and four smaller powers which were elected by the Assembly.

(ii) The *Assembly* — all countries attended the Assembly which met once a year. Each country, no matter the size, had an equal vote.

(iii) *International Court of Justice* — a group of judges could be called upon to settle disputes.

(iv) *Auxiliary bodies* — groups like the International Labour Organisation, for example, to improve working conditions.

League membership was open to all countries except the defeated nations of World War One. As a result

(i) Germany, Austria, Hungary, Bulgaria and Turkey were denied immediate membership. However, by 1926 all had been admitted.

(ii) The USSR remained outside the League.

(iii) The American Senate, by seven votes, did not give Woodrow Wilson the power to make the USA a member.

Weaknesses of the League

(i) The *absence of America* was a serious blow to the prestige and influence of the League.

(ii) Close links with the Treaty of Versailles meant that Germany, even though a member in 1926, viewed it with suspicion.

(iii) Articles of the League (Covenant of the League) were vague in that

(a) military sanctions did not appear to exist since the League did not have an army,

(b) economic sanctions seemed to be the strongest sanction available but this could be slow and difficult to operate.

Nonetheless, the League did have some success in the 1920s by solving disputes between countries without war starting.

The search for security through disarmament

After the horrors of World War One, politicians were under pressure to bring about disarmament. A Disarmament Conference did not take place in the 1920s because there was not enough agreement between countries. In particular, the following were obstacles to disarmament through the League.

(i) The attitude of France — the French did not believe that the League's articles were sufficiently strong to provide collective security. Consequently, France made alliances with countries like Belgium, Poland, Czechoslovakia and Romania. She did not feel sufficiently confident in the League to disarm.

(ii) The attitude of Britain — In 1922 and 1924, British governments opposed attempts by the League to strengthen its Articles. By these proposals, if countries disarmed then all other countries in the League would come to the aid of the attacked country. The opposition of Britain meant that the articles were not strengthened and disarmament did not follow.

Disarmament did not take place through the League in the twenties although conferences outside the League achieved

(i) a measure of naval disarmament at the Washington Treaty of 1922. Navies of the major powers of America, Britain and Japan were fixed at the ratio of 5:5:3.

(ii) a fairly meaningless agreement was signed in 1928 by over sixty countries called the Kellogg-Briand Pact. The countries who signed it claimed to renounce war as an instrument of national policy.

It was not until 1931 that the League found sufficient agreement amongst nations to proceed with a Disarmament Conference. With the rise of Hitler to power in Germany, in 1933, the Conference was doomed to failure. In 1934 it collapsed, and countries started to rearm.

UNIT 3 — People and Power

CONTEXT C: Russia 1914–1941

PART ONE — 1914–1917

1

Nature of the Tsarist Government

1. *Autocracy*

   (a) In 1914, Russia's Government was a form of autocracy. This meant that power was exercised by the Tsar with the help of his ministers. However, he could make decisions without listening to anyone else.

   (b) After the 1905 Revolution, a Duma (Parliament) had been granted by the Tsar. However, it was very weak and unsuccessful. This was because

      (i) the electoral laws had been altered to make it easier for the supporters of the Tsar to be elected rather than opponents;

      (ii) the Tsar did not want to share any of his power with the Duma.

2. *The Romanovs*

   (a) Tsar Nicholas II was the head of the Russian Empire in 1914. He was a weak and indecisive person. He found it very difficult to tell people unpleasant news to their face. Instead, he would prefer to write them a letter.

   (b) Nicholas was not interested in the daily work of a ruler, he found it boring.

   (c) In 1895, Nicholas said "I shall preserve the principle of autocracy just as firmly . . . as my late, unforgettable father preserved it!"

   (d) Nicholas's German wife, Alexandra, was a firm supporter of the autocracy. She dominated her husband and encouraged him to retain all his power.

(e) Nicholas had five children. The youngest and only male child, Alexis, was the heir to the throne (the Tsarevitch). He suffered from a blood disease called haemophilia. This prevented the blood from clotting and meant that Alexis's life was constantly at risk. This problem often distracted the Tsar from other affairs.

3. *The Empire*

   (a) About 125 million people lived in the Russian Empire.

   (b) There were around twenty different nationalities within the Empire. Each had their own language and customs. Many did not speak Russian.

   (c) The Empire covered a vast area. Approximately 5,700 miles separates the Western and Eastern extremities of this land. It took ten days to travel this distance by train.

Obviously the Tsar could not control this Empire by himself. He needed supporters to help him govern.

4. *The Tsar's Supporters*

   (a) The Nobility
      (i) Their wealth came from the land. They owned 25% of the land but were only 1% of the population.
      (ii) They controlled the peasants on their estates.

   (b) The Civil Service
      (i) Collected taxes from the people and enforced the Tsar's decisions.
      (ii) Were often very corrupt and could be bribed.
      (iii) The Civil Service was inefficient.

   (c) The Okhrana (Secret Police)
      (i) Censored all books and newspapers.
      (ii) Arrested opponents of the Tsar.
      (iii) People arrested by the Okhrana were often exiled to Siberia.

(d) The Army

   (i) Used to restore order and crush revolts. Cossacks were the most feared group of soldiers.

   (ii) Officers were usually from the nobility.

(e) The Russian Orthodox Church

   (i) Taught people to respect the Tsar and obey him.

   (ii) The Head of the Church was a government minister. Bishops took orders from him and passed on instructions to the priests. This meant that the Government could control what was said in Church.

All of these groups supported the Tsar. This was because they enjoyed much wealth and power under the Tsarist autocracy. However, many people were opposed to the Tsar because

(a) they wanted more power,

(b) they wanted to improve their standard of living,

(c) they wanted to change the government.

2

Discontent Under the Tsar Arising From Economic Hardship, Political Opposition and the Effects of the First World War

1. **Economic Hardship**

(a) *Peasants* formed 80% of the population in 1900. They were heavily taxed to pay for the process of industrialisation in Russia. They suffered from a shortage of land and backward agricultural techniques. Poor harvests and famines were common. Peasants often lived in one-roomed huts which they shared with their livestock. The result of these hardships was a great deal of discontent among the peasantry. This can clearly be seen in events such as the peasant uprisings during the 1905 Revolution.

(b) *Industrial workers* formed around 15% of the population. Many were peasants who had moved to the cities for work. They worked long hours for low pay. They had poor living conditions. Many slept in either overcrowded dormitories or barracks. Many accidents took place because of poor working conditions. Discontent among workers was common with strikes a regular occurrence.

2. Political Opposition

    (a) Constitutional Democrats (Kadets). This was a Liberal party which wanted to see a government very similar to the one in Britain. This would mean the Tsar losing much of his power. This group was supported by many people from the middle classes.

    (b) Social Revolutionaries wanted to take the land from the Tsar and landowners and give it to the peasants. Supported by peasants.

    (c) Social Democrats. This group followed the ideas of Karl Marx. He believed that the factory owners (the Capitalist class) exploited the workers (the Proletariat) by giving them low wages and poor working conditions. Eventually, the situation would become so bad that the workers would revolt. They would seize power after two revolutions.

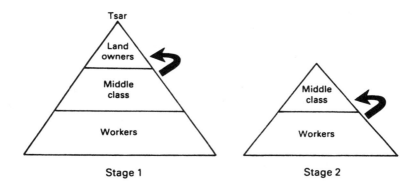

These revolutions would take place in an industrialised country.

By 1914, the Social Democrats had split into two groups, Mensheviks and Bolsheviks. They disagreed on the best way of starting a revolution.

(a) Mensheviks

    (i)   Mass party of trade unionists.

    (ii) Emphasis on open work and activities which would not upset the Okhrana.

    (iii) In favour of peaceful change.

(b) *Bolsheviks* — led by Vladimir Ilyich Ulyanov (Lenin).

   (i) Small party of disciplined revolutionaries.

   (ii) Emphasis on secrecy to outwit the Okhrana.

   (iii) Prepared to use violence.

The Bolsheviks, led by Lenin, felt that the Menshevik plan was too slow — it would never lead to a revolution. Both groups attracted the support of the working classes.

3. **The Effects of the First World War**

In August, 1914, Russia entered the Great War. At first the war united the population against the common enemy — Germany. The capital of the Tsarist Empire, St. Petersburg, changed its name to Petrograd. This was because its original name sounded too German.

The political parties in the Duma declared an end to opposition politics for the duration of the war. However, this unity was short-lived for several reasons.

(a) *Military defeats* at Tannenberg (August 1914) and Masurian Lakes (September 1914) cost 250,000 men. By the end of 1914, one million men had become casualties. These disasters continued through the war and were caused by

   (i) Poor leaders — many officers lacked proper training.

   (ii) Poor tactics — officers did not understand the effects of new weapons such as the machine gun.

   (iii) A shortage of equipment such as rifles and ammunition.

(b) *Collapse of the Economy* was caused by several factors.

   (i) Workers — 15·5 million men went to the army. Many factories had to close because they could not get enough workers. Many farms did not have enough people to work the land.

(ii) Transport — There was not enough trains to transport essential supplies around the country. This led to shortages in some parts of the country while thousands of tonnes of material rotted in other areas. Many factories had to close because they could not get supplies.

(iii) Inflation — Food prices rose faster than wages. This meant that people could afford less.

(c) The Royal Family

(i) In 1915, the Tsar assumed control of the Russian armies. This meant that he could now be directly blamed for any defeats.

(ii) Tsarina Alexandra was left in charge. She was unpopular with the ordinary people and was seen as a German spy.

Alexandra was able to do as she pleased. She changed ministers who disagreed with her. During a period of 16 months there were

(i) four different Prime Ministers,

(ii) five different Ministers of the Interior,

(iii) four different Ministers of Agriculture,

(iv) three different Ministers of War,

(v) two different Ministers of Foreign Affairs.

This was known as 'ministerial leapfrog'. It led to the work of the Government grinding to a halt.

(d) Rasputin

(i) He was a monk or holy man who, due to his apparent power to make the Tsarevitch feel better, had a great deal of influence over Alexandra.

(ii) He used this influence to bring his own friends into positions of power.

(iii) He was hated by the population, who saw him as a drunkard, womaniser and a corrupt influence. The nobles were jealous of his power while the rest saw him as damaging the Russian war effort.

(iv) He was murdered in December 1916 by several members of the nobility. However, it came too late to improve the Tsarist conduct of the war.

These factors not only altered the shape of the Tsarist Government, they also provoked discontent amongst the population.

(e) *The Effects of the War on the Civilian Population*

By February 1917, people were unhappy because

(i) it was winter and they were unable to get fuel because of the collapse of the railways,

(ii) there was a shortage of food,

(iii) high casualties in the war,

(iv) the conduct of the royal family.

3

The February Revolution of 1917

These factors resulted in a *spontaneous* outbreak of demonstrations and disorder.

It is important to remember that Russia used a different calendar at this time. It was thirteen days behind the rest of Europe. As a result, the February revolution is also known as the March revolution.

1. Wednesday, 22nd February.
   Workers at Putilov works go on strike after failure of pay talks.

2. Thursday, 23rd February.
   (a) 90,000 workers on strike.
   (b) Demonstrations about the shortage of bread.

3. Friday, 24th February.
   200,000 workers demonstrating. Police and army used to control them.

4. Saturday, 25th February.
   250,000 workers demonstrating. Troops fire on processions.

5. Sunday, 26th February.
   (a) Government loses control on streets. Troops firing at each other.
   (b) Tsar warned of serious situation. Orders Duma to stop meeting.

6. Monday, 27th February.
   (a) Volinsky army regiment mutinies and supports demonstrations.
   (b) Despite Tsar's orders, Duma meets and sets up Provisional Committee to take over the Government.
   (c) Revolutionaries set up a Soviet (council) of workers and soldiers. It is supposed to take over the Government and organise food supplies.

7. Tuesday, 28th February.
   Tsar offers to share power with Duma. Told that it was too late.

8. Wednesday, 1st March.
   (a) Generals inform Tsar that army no longer supports him.
   (b) Tsar is prevented by revolutionaries from returning to Petrograd.

9. Thursday, 2nd March.
   (a) Tsar agrees to abdicate (give up the throne).
   (b) Refuses to allow Alexis to replace him as Tsar because of his illness.
   (c) Crown offered to Grand Duke Michael. However, he fears that he will simply become unpopular and refuses.

Results of the February Revolution

(a) Russia was no longer an autocracy.

(b) There were two rival organisations competing for power.
   (i) The Provisional Government composed of middle class Liberal policies.
   (ii) The Soviet composed of workers and soldiers' deputies.

Both, initially, met in the Tauride Palace, in Petrograd. The Provisional Government eventually moved to the Winter Palace.

PART 2 — 1917–1924

4

The Formation and Characteristics of the Provisional Government

This was formed of middle class liberal politicians. It was supposed to govern Russia until elections to a constituent assembly (Parliament) could be organised. There were four Provisional Governments between February and October 1917. They had many problems to deal with. However, they often tried to avoid important decisions as they felt none should be made until after the elections. They did introduce some important reforms.

1. All the Tsarist Governors were removed from office. They were replaced by people with no experience of administration. The new Government felt it could not trust bureaucrats associated with the Tsar. This decision was to prove a mistake.

2. The Department of Police and Okhrana were abolished. This was a popular decision; however, it meant there was no force the Government could rely on.

3. The death penalty was abolished.

4. Freedom of speech was allowed. This was popular, but also meant criticism of the Government.

5. Political prisoners were freed and an amnesty to all opponents of the Tsar was issued.

6. Poland was promised full independence after the war. Finland was promised that her constitutional rights would be restored. (Poland and Finland were part of Russia at this time.) Both of these promises were popular with people in these areas.

The Provisional Governments could not make decisions on their own. They had to share power with the Soviet. Indeed, this assembly of workers and soldiers' deputies had more influence over many areas of everyday life. This can be seen with Order Number One:

   (i) Committees were elected in each unit to replace officers.

  (ii) These committees controlled arms, ammunition and equipment.

 (iii) Officers were not to be saluted.

 (iv) All soldiers and sailors were to obey the Soviet.

This order was obeyed by all sections of the armed forces. It demonstrated that the army and navy were under the control of the Soviet. The Provisional Government had no real power to back up its decisions. It had to rely on the Soviet, which also controlled the railway, postal and telegraph services. This meant the Government had to listen to the Soviet.

5

Discontent Under the Provisional Government

1. Continuation of the War

The Provisional Government decided to continue to support Britain and France against Germany. This was mainly because

(a) They did not wish to upset their allies by making peace. Russia needed large sums of money, and much of this came from the west. Britain and France might withdraw investment if Russia pulled out of the war.

(b) The Government was afraid of the demands Germany might place on Russia.

(c) Many people in the Government, such as Alexander Kerensky (Prime Minister, July–October 1917), felt that a victorious war would unite the people behind the Government.

The decision to remain in the war was unpopular and caused discontent. This was seen in April 1917. The Provisional Government sent a note to the allies telling them they would continue in the war. However, this telegram upset many people. It appeared the Government was continuing in the war so that it could gain land, not just defend Russia from Germany. As a result:

(a) There were riots and disorder by soldiers and civilians against the Government.

(b) It was the Soviet who restored order, not the Government or army.

(c) The Foreign Minister who sent the note to the allies, Paul Miliukov, resigned.

(d) Members of the Soviet leadership entered into a coalition Government with members of the previous Provisional Government. This meant that they would now also be blamed for any future setbacks.

In June 1917, a new Russian offensive failed with heavy casualties. Many soldiers deserted. This resulted in more discontent being directed at the Government.

2. Failure to solve economic and social problems

(a) *Demands for Bread* — The Provisional Government did little to improve the supply of food to the major cities such as Moscow and Petrograd. There were continual shortages throughout 1917. The price of food rose much faster than wages. There was much discontent over this issue and food riots were common.

(b)   *Demands for Land* — Little progress was made in tackling the land problem. The Government wanted to wait until after elections to the Constituent Assembly to decide the matter. This meant that the peasants became discontented with the Government. It also ignored reality. After the February revolution, many peasants had simply seized the land.

The Constituent Assembly

Little progress was made in organising elections. This was possibly because the Provisional Government felt it had more important problems to deal with. However, it caused discontent amongst the population who wanted to elect a Government it supported.

6

Lenin's Return to Russia, the July Days and Kornilov Revolt

Lenin's return

One of the first actions of the Provisional Government was to grant a political amnesty to former opponents of the Tsar. Many such as Lenin returned to cause problems for the Government.

Lenin and the Bolsheviks were not members or supporters of the Provisional Government. In fact, Lenin did not believe that the Soviet should co-operate with the Government. As a result, neither he nor the Bolsheviks were the target of popular discontent.

Lenin was in exile in Switzerland in February 1917. He had moved there to escape the Tsarist police. He returned to Russia with the help of the Germans. They wanted him to start another revolution which would knock Russia out of the war. After Lenin's return to Petrograd, he announced his plans. These became known as the *April Theses*. They meant:

(a) An end to Russia's involvement with the war.

(b) Land to be given to the peasants.

(c) Control of factories to be given to the workers.

(d) Banks to be nationalised.

(e) No support for the Provisional Government. Instead, the Soviets would form the basis of the new Government.

Popular Bolshevik slogans were 'All Power to the Soviets' and 'Peace, Bread and Land'! With the April Theses, Lenin hoped to gain support from the people by promising them what they wanted.

The July Days

1. In July 1917, the Government ordered troops from Petrograd to go to the front. They refused, and men of the 1st Machine Gun Regiment mutinied. They had been subjected to Bolshevik propaganda. As a result, they used Bolshevik slogans such as 'All Power to the Soviets'.

2. The soldiers were joined by workers and sailors who were unhappy with the Provisional Government's policies. They supported the ideas of Lenin and the Bolsheviks.

3. Controversy exists between historians over the role of the Bolsheviks in the July Days. Many claim the Bolsheviks did not plan the uprising, but felt they had to join it when the demonstrators used their slogans. However, some claim that it was a planned uprising and attempt to seize power by the Bolsheviks. Either way, it failed when loyal troops were brought to Petrograd. Four hundred people were killed.

4. This uprising had several results.

    (a) Lenin fled to Finland.

    (b) The Provisional Government made public evidence linking Lenin with the Germans. Kerensky attempted to prove that Lenin was a German agent and so discredit the Bolsheviks. It was shown that Lenin had returned to Russia with German help. This lost Lenin some supporters.

    (c) The Bolshevik party was thrown into disarray. Many members went into hiding and others were arrested.

The Kornilov Revolt

General Lavr Kornilov was the Commander-in-Chief of the Russian army after July 1917. He became discontented with the Provisional Government because

(a) Order No. 1 and the military committees had led to the collapse of discipline in the army. Kornilov wanted the reintroduction of the death penalty to restore order.

(b) The war was not being run successfully. Kornilov wanted to march on Petrograd and

    (i) destroy the Soviet and arrest all the Socialists,

    (ii) assume control of the Provisional Government and reorganise the war effort.

He hoped that this would allow the war to be conducted much more successfully.

In September 1917, he ordered his troops to march on Petrograd and seize power. Unfortunately for Kornilov and the Provisional Government, the plan backfired.

(a) Kornilov's troops (the 'Savage' Division and the Cossacks) refused to attack the Provisional Government, Kornilov was arrested.

(b) As Kerensky had so few loyal troops, he armed the Bolsheviks. Red Guard detachments were set up to defend the city. It was these groups who received credit for saving Russia. Many people began supporting the Bolsheviks after the Kornilov revolt.

The Bolsheviks after September 1917 now had

  (i) armed units under their control,

  (ii) public support.

7

The October Revolution, 1917

A   *Causes*

There was a second revolution in October 1917, because

(a) The Provisional Government failed

    (i) to end the war,

    (ii) to solve problems of food shortages and rising prices,

    (iii) to solve the land problem,

    (iv) to organise elections for the Constituent Assembly.

This led to discontent amongst the ordinary people, who started to support the Bolsheviks. This was because Lenin promised 'Peace, Bread and Land'. By late September 1917, the Bolsheviks controlled the Petrograd and Moscow Soviets.

(b) The Provisional Governments were shown to be powerless because

    (i) they could not prevent peasants from seizing the land,

    (ii) they could not prevent soldiers from deserting,

    (iii) they had to rely on their enemies, the Bolsheviks, to protect them from Kornilov,

    (iv) they had no popular support because they had not been elected.

These factors encouraged Lenin to seize power. From mid-September, he wrote letters to the Central Committee urging them to seize power. However, it was not until 10th October that he attended a committee meeting and persuaded them to seize power.

B *Preparations*

Leon Trotsky was put in charge of organising the Bolshevik seizure of power.

(a) He convinced the Petrograd Soviet to set up a Military Revolutionary Committee (MRC). This was controlled by the Bolsheviks. It took charge of co-ordinating the attack on the Government. It instructed army units not to obey instructions unless they were countersigned by the MRC. This meant that the Provisional Government lost its authority over many troops.

(b) Commissars were sent to the army units in Petrograd. These were supporters of the Bolsheviks. They were supposed to make sure that the Soviets' instructions were followed.

(c) Trotsky convinced those troops who were not supporters of the Bolsheviks to stay neutral. He was very successful. Only 4% of the garrison supported the Bolsheviks. However, even less supported the Government. The rest stayed in their barracks during the uprising.

(d) The workers were equipped with weapons from the Peter and Paul fortress. Meetings were organised to raise support for the Bolsheviks amongst the factory workers.

(e) Bolshevik headquarters were set up in the Smolny Institute. This was a disused girls' school.

C   *The Attack*

On the night of the 24th and the morning of the 25th October 1917, the Bolsheviks seized important points around the capital. These were:

(a) Bridges over the River Neva — to prevent loyal troops helping the Provisional Government.

(b) Communications centres such as the Head Post Office, Telegraph Station and the Telephone Exchange — to prevent the Government asking for help.

(c) Railway Stations — to prevent the arrival of loyal troops in Petrograd.

(d) Important Government buildings such as the State Bank.

(e) The Power Station.

By the evening of 25th October, only the Winter Palace, home for the Provisional Government, was still holding out against the Bolsheviks. At 9 p.m., the cruiser *Aurora* sailed up the River Neva and fired a salvo of blank shells at the Winter Palace. It did not have any live shells. At 11 p.m., the Peter and Paul fortress opened fire on the Palace. However, only two of its shells struck, causing little damage. Yet by midnight, most of the defenders had lost heart and had left the building. Only the 'Women's Battalion of Death' (a unit set up in 1917 by the Government to shame men into fighting the Germans) and a small group of young officer cadets were still guarding the Government. In the early hours of 26th October, small groups of soldiers and Red Guards entered the building without much resistance. At 2.10 a.m., the ministers of the Provisional Government were all arrested. This was with the exception of Kerensky, who had escaped and was trying to find loyal troops to suppress the revolt.

By 26th October, Lenin was able to announce in the All Russian Congress of Soviets that power had been seized. The Bolsheviks were now in control of Petrograd. They had managed to seize power without too much bloodshed. Only five people had been killed during the capture of the Winter Palace. It was a very different story in Moscow, where the Bolsheviks were only able to take power after several days of heavy fighting. The Bolsheviks now controlled Petrograd and Moscow. However, large parts of Russia were not controlled.

8

The Bolshevik Government

Bolshevik Government under Lenin, 1917–1924

To enable the Bolsheviks to govern Russia, a Council of Peoples Commissars (Sovnarkom) was set up in October 1917. This immediately began issuing decrees which would either gain the support of the population or attack opponents.

1. *Decrees Gaining Support*

   (a) 26th October 1917 — *Peace*

   This said that Russia would make peace with the Central Powers immediately. This would please most people, especially soldiers and sailors.

   (b) 26th October 1917 — *Land*

   The peasants were to be given land taken from the Tsar and other landowners. In reality, the peasants had already seized the land. However, it did avoid conflict with the new Government. This decree was based on ideas taken from the Socialist Revolutionary Party who were very popular with the peasants.

   (c) 31st October 1917 — *Work*

   An eight-hour day was introduced for all workers.

   (d) 1st November 1917 — *Unemployment Insurance*

   Unemployment insurance was promised to all workers who were sick or unemployed.

   (e) 14th December 1917 — *Factories*

   These were put under the control of workers' committees.

   (f) 14th December 1917 — *Banks*

   Banks were put under Sovnarkoms control.

It was hoped that these decrees would help make Russian society much fairer, as well as gaining support for the Bolsheviks. Other reforms were introduced to help achieve this objective. Women were given equal rights with men and all ranks and titles were abolished. Everyone was to be called Comrade. However, before this improved society could be reached, opponents of Lenin and the Bolsheviks had to be destroyed.

2. *Decrees Attacking Opponents*

   (a) 27th October 1917 — *Newspapers*
   Those which did not support the Bolsheviks were banned.

   (b) 28th November 1917 — *The Kadets* (Constitutional Democratic Party)
   The main Liberal party in Russia was banned.

   (c) 7th December 1917 — *The CHEKA* ('All-Russian Extraordinary Commission to fight Counter-Revolution and Espionage')
   This was set up and was a police force designed to attack opponents of Lenin.

3. *The Constituent Assembly*

   The Provisional Government had promised elections to the Constituent Assembly. The Bolsheviks could not prevent them from being carried out. The results were very unsatisfactory for the Bolsheviks. Out of 707 seats they won 175. The Socialist Revolutionaries won 370 of the seats and were the largest party. The Bolsheviks responded by closing the assembly in January 1918, and refusing to allow it to reopen. They claimed they did not need it as they had the 'Congress of Soviets'. This was dominated by the Bolsheviks. By mid-1918, Russia was proclaimed as a one-party state. This meant there could be no opposition.

4. *The Treaty of Brest-Litovsk*

   Lenin demanded that Russia had to be pulled out of the war. He sent Trotsky to try and make peace with the Germans. Trotsky hoped that, before any treaty was signed, a revolution would break out in Germany. It did not. Eventually, the Bolsheviks signed the Treaty of Brest-Litovsk in March 1918. Its terms were very harsh. Russia lost

   (a) 26% of her population,
   (b) 27% of her farmland,
   (c) 26% of her railways,
   (d) 74% of her coal and iron ore output,
   (e) 300 million roubles to the Germans,
   (f) Poland, Latvia, Lithuania, Estonia, Finland and the Ukraine.

   This treaty allowed Russia to stop fighting in the Great War. However, it upset many Russians because of its harsh terms. It also annoyed the British and French. They had wanted the Russians to continue in the war against the Germans. Now the Allies feared the Germans would be able to transfer their troops from the Eastern to the Western Front.

9

Civil War Between the Bolsheviks and the White Armies

The Civil War

This was fought between the Bolsheviks (Reds) and their opponents (Whites) between 1918–1922. It was a struggle for control over Russia.

The White Forces

This was the term used to describe all opponents of Bolshevism during the civil war. White was the traditional colour for supporters of the Tsar. However, not all 'Whites' would support the Tsar. In fact, a common dislike of Lenin and the Bolsheviks was about all that many had in common.

1. *The Czech Legion*

   Around 40 000 soldiers were being transported to Vladivostock along the Trans-Siberian Railway. They wanted to get to the Western front to continue the war against Germany. However, before they could leave, they quarrelled with the Bolsheviks. This led to them seizing most of the railway line and attacking the Reds. The formation of the new state of Czechoslovakia (October 1918) and the end of the Great War (November 1918) increased their desire to leave. They eventually left in April 1920.

2. *Supporters of the Tsar*

   A very small group that wanted the return of the autocracy.

3. *Kadets*

   Middle class Liberals who wanted a democracy similar to Britain.

4. *Social Revolutionaries and Mensheviks*

   Disagreed with Bolsheviks over November Revolution and the Constituent Assembly.

5. *Landowners, factory owners and businessmen*

   Wanted the return of land, factories and businesses which the Bolsheviks had seized. Provided money for Whites.

6. *Ex-Tsarist Officers*

These opposed the Bolsheviks and were unhappy with the Treaty of Brest-Litovsk. They formed armies led by

(a) General Yudenich in Estonia,
(b) Admiral Kolchak in Siberia,
(c) General Denikin in the South. He was later replaced by General Wrangel.

7. *Cossacks*

Formed much of the volunteer armies.

8. *Interventionist Powers*

The Allied Powers, Britain, France, USA and Japan, all sent troops to Russia. They did this for several reasons.

(a) To protect valuable war materials which had been transported to Russia.
(b) To force Russia to restart their involvement in the Great War.
(c) To prevent the spread of Communism after the end of the Great War.
(d) Japan sent troops in an attempt to increase influence in Siberia.

The Red Forces

1. Leon Trotsky was in charge of the Red Army. He held the positions of Commissar for War and Chairman of the Supreme War Council.

2. Trotsky played an important part in leading the Red Army. He moved around the front line in a train. This carried troops and supplies which Trotsky was able to take to critical areas and give help to areas which needed it.

3. The Red Army was conscripted in areas controlled by the Bolsheviks. At the height of the war it was five million strong.

4. Around 50 000 ex-Tsarist army officers were used to command the army. Their families were taken as hostages to make sure they co-operated.

5. Dedicated Bolsheviks were appointed as Commissars. They shared authority with officers and were able to ensure their loyalty.

6. Strict discipline was reintroduced. Desertion, throwing away equipment and refusing to carry out orders were punishable by death.

7. To help maintain discipline within Bolshevik areas, the CHEKA started a Red Terror. Opponents were arrested and executed.

Factors behind the Red Army's success in the Civil War

Before the fighting began, the Whites had more advantages than the Reds.

(a) More men and officers from the Tsarist army.
(b) Controlled food-producing areas (except Ukraine).
(c) Much support from foreign powers.

However, by 1922, the Red Army were the victors. This was for a variety of reasons.

1. *Communications*

   The Reds controlled a central area which had good railway lines. They were able to move troops around the fronts much more easily than the Whites.

2. *Leadership*

   Lenin and Trotsky controlled the Red Army. There was little co-operation between the White Generals. This meant that they did not attack the Bolsheviks all at once.

3. *Motivation*

   The Red Army was fighting for the Bolshevik party. Defeat meant death. The Whites were fighting for a variety of different reasons and often disagreed amongst themselves.

4. *Foreign Support*

   (a) After 1919, the end of the Great War, the Allies began to pull out of Russia. Their role in the civil war was unpopular amongst their own people.
   (b) Foreign intervention was seen as an invasion of Russia by the population. This led many of them to support the Bolsheviks, who were portrayed as the defenders of Russia.

5. *Propaganda*

   Both sides made use of propaganda to win support.

   (a) The Bolsheviks told the peasants that if the Whites were victorious, then the land would be taken away from them. This convinced many to support the Bolsheviks.
   (b) In July 1918, the Royal Family were murdered in Ekaterinburg. This was because the Bolsheviks were afraid that the Tsar might be freed by the advancing Czech Legion. They did not want him to become a focus of discontent against the Bolsheviks. As a result, Nicholas and his family were shot and their bodies destroyed. This provided the White forces with propaganda. However, it was not very effective within Russia as the Tsar was unpopular.

The Effects of the Civil War on the Peasants

1. The war caused a great deal of suffering among the peasants.

2. Many of their villages and homes were destroyed during the civil war.

3. Much of their food and livestock were seized by both Red and White armies.

4. The introduction of War Communism increased this suffering.

5. Some peasants reacted by becoming Partisans who attacked both Red and White armies.

10

Activities of the Bolshevik Government under Lenin as Demonstrated by War Communism

War Communism

This was introduced for two reasons.

1. To make sure the Red Army was kept supplied with food and weapons.

2. To try and introduce some of the most important aspects of Communism.

War Communism meant

1. All factories of more than ten workers were nationalised. The Bolsheviks set up Vesenkha (The Supreme Council of National Economy) to tell each factory what to produce.

2. Workers were conscripted to work in the factories. They were given work books which allowed them to buy food and clothes. Strict discipline was enforced. Workers who went on strike could be executed.

3. Private trade was forbidden. Surplus crops were supposed to be given to the Bolshevik Government at a fixed price.

4. Money became valueless. People had to barter for goods.

5. Food was rationed.

War Communism was very unpopular and led to a lot of discontent.

11

Reasons why War Communism led to Discontent

1. *Peasants*

   They disliked War Communism because they were forced to hand over their crops to the Government. If they refused they were shot. The Communists sent requisition squads into the countryside to seize crops. The peasants reacted by growing less grain. They did not see the point. The result was a famine in 1921 which led to the deaths of 7·5 million people.

2. *Working Class*

   This group was unhappy with War Communism because it did not solve the problems affecting them. Food was in short supply. Many workers went on strike to protest about this. Many others left the towns for the countryside where they hoped to find food. Between 1917 and 1920, the working class in towns fell from 2·6 million to 1·2 million. This worried the Communists, as this group provided much of their support. The workers who remained in the towns were subjected to strict discipline; absenteeism was dealt with very severely. The working day was lengthened to ten or eleven hours.

12

Activities of the Bolshevik Government under Lenin as Demonstrated by the New Economic Policy

The New Economic Policy

This was introduced in March 1921, to replace War Communism. It meant

(a) Requisitions were ended. Peasants had to pay a tax in kind (grain). After 1924 this became a money tax. Surplus grain could be sold by the peasants for a profit.

(b) Industries of less than twenty workers were given back to their original owners. It was thought they would work hard to make a profit.

(c) The currency was stabilised.

(d) The Communists retained control of important industries (coal, iron, steel, oil, electricity and the railways). These were described as the 'commanding heights of industry' by Lenin.

Results of the New Economic Policy (NEP)

1. Agricultural output increased. By 1925 it had reached pre-war levels. Rich peasants (Kulaks) did particularly well. After 1925, they could hire labour to help on the farms. Thus, the most important objective of NEP was achieved.

2. Light industry benefited from an increased demand for consumer goods by the peasants.

3. NEP men became common. These people acted as 'middle men' between the town and countryside. They brought consumer goods to the countryside which they sold at a profit to the peasants. They returned to the towns with food which they could also sell at a profit.

4. Heavy industry did not recover.

Opposition to the New Economic Policy

Many 'Old Bolsheviks' were unhappy with the NEP. They felt that it was a step backwards away from Marxism and the Communist state. However, Lenin claimed that it was necessary to save the revolution. He believed that the Communist Government could not survive unless it regained the support of the peasantry.

Constitution of 1923

1. Russia became known as the Union of Soviet Socialist Republics.

2. The country was a union of four republics — Russia, Byelorussia, the Ukraine and the Caucasus.

3. Each republic had control over health, welfare and education.

4. Sovnarkom controlled the armed forces, industry, communications and the CHEKA.

PART 3

RUSSIA 1924–1941

13

Activities of the Communist Government under Stalin as Demonstrated by the Five Year Plans

Lenin's Death

In January 1924, Lenin died. He had been severely wounded by shots fired by Fanya Kaplan, a Left-wing Social Revolutionary, in August 1918. Although he recovered, his health went into decline. In 1922 and 1923, he suffered a series of strokes which gradually robbed him of his powers of speech. Lenin died in January 1924. His body was embalmed and put on display in the Kremlin. His death led to problems concerning the leadership of the Soviet Union. There were two main rivals for the leadership, Leon Trotsky and Joseph Stalin. Lenin preferred Trotsky to be his successor as he believed Stalin was 'too rude'. However, Lenin died before he could ensure Trotsky's succession.

Joseph Stalin

Born in Tiflis, Georgia, in 1879, Stalin joined the Social Democratic Party in 1898. After 1903, he sided with the Bolsheviks and was responsible for the organisation of strikes and raising funds for the party. The last task involved him in leading bank robberies and protection rackets. Despite later claims, Stalin did not play a prominent role in the October Revolution of 1917. He was, however, a leading Bolshevik and did play an important part in the Civil War.

Stalin's rise to power — Background

Stalin's struggle to become sole leader of the Communist party was intertwined with his plans to industrialise the Soviet Union. His rise to power also demonstrates how ruthless he could be in purging opposition within the party.

1. *General Secretary of the Communist Party* — Stalin was appointed to this post in 1922. This allowed him to appoint his supporters to various positions in the Communist Party.

2. *Lenin's death in 1924*

   (a) Prevented Stalin's removal by Lenin. Lenin's 'Testament', in which he criticised Stalin and advised his removal as General Secretary, was ignored.

   (b) Stalin made the arrangements for Lenin's funeral and read the oration. To the public it appeared that the two had been very close and that Stalin was the natural successor.

   (c) Trotsky did not attend the funeral. He claimed that Stalin had not informed him of the date.

3. *The Defeat of Trotsky (1924–1925)*

   The struggle between Trotsky and Stalin centred on the future development of the USSR. There were two alternatives.

   (a) *World Revolution* (also known as permanent revolution). This idea was supported by Trotsky. He believed that Russia could not defend herself from attack by other capitalist powers. Trotsky wanted to export revolution to other countries. He hoped this would lead to uprisings by the working class, who would overthrow their governments and help the Soviet Union.

   (b) *Socialism in One Country*. This idea was supported by Stalin. He believed that industry and agriculture had to be developed within the Soviet Union. Only then would Communism be safe.

   By 1925, Stalin had convinced the Communist Party to support his policy. This was achieved because

   (a) Stalin sent Trotsky's supporters to distant parts of the USSR where they could not influence the debate.

   (b) Trotsky was unpopular because he was Jewish and had not always been a Bolshevik. He had originally been a Menshevik.

   (c) Many Communists feared that the West was about to attack the USSR.

   At the 1925 Party Congress, Trotsky lost his position as Commissar for War. In 1927, he was expelled from the Communist Party. In 1929, he was forced to leave the USSR. Finally, Stalin had Trotsky murdered in 1940. By this time Trotsky was living in Mexico. A member of the NKVD struck him on the head with an ice pick. Trotsky was writing a biography of Stalin at the time. Thus, Stalin disposed of one of his chief rivals.

4. *The Defeat of the Left Opposition*

This was a group of Communists who wanted the end of NEP. The best known were Kamenev and Zinoviev. Stalin defeated them with the support of the 'Right Opposition' and had them removed from positions within the party. They were replaced by supporters of Stalin.

5. *The Defeat of the Right Opposition*

This was a group of Communists who wished to continue with NEP as long as it continued to meet the nation's food needs. The best known was Bukharin, an economic theorist and a leading member of the Communist Party.

Stalin defeated them by

(a) Arguing that the West was about to attack. NEP had to end and industrialisation had to begin. Otherwise, the USSR would be destroyed.

(b) Arguing that there was a grain shortage. Agriculture had to be collectivised.

(c) Removing supporters of the Right Opposition and replacing them with Stalinists.

(d) By 1929, the Right Opposition had been defeated and lost all their important positions. However, they were allowed to remain in the Communist party. Bukharin was shot during the purges in 1938.

By 1929, Stalin was the undisputed leader of the Communist party. He had destroyed all forms of opposition within the party and could now concentrate on his policy of 'Socialism in one country'.

Stalin's 'Socialism in One Country'

This policy involved
1. Industrialisation of the Soviet Union through Five Year Plans.
2. Collectivisation of agriculture.

Stalin was in overall charge of the transformation of the USSR.

The Five Year Plans — Industrialisation of the Soviet Union

(a) Reasons for rapid industrialisation

(i) USSR had to be able to defend itself from attack by Western Powers.

(ii) In the late twenties, the Soviet Union was not regarded as possessing enough heavy industry to produce weapons. This situation had to be improved. NEP was not the answer.

(iii) In 1927, there was a 'War Scare'. Stalin claimed the West was about to invade. The assault never came. However, it was thought likely that the Soviet Union would be attacked within ten years. For this reason, the USSR had to be industrialised as quickly as possible.

(b) Organisation

(i) Stalin was in overall charge of the process. He controlled Gosplan (the State Planning Commission). This issued targets which had to be met for industry and agriculture. These targets were incorporated into 'Five Year Plans'. Each had a different emphasis. These figures were often very unrealistic. However, managers and workers were put under pressure to meet them. If they failed they could be arrested and executed. This was known as the Command Economy.

(ii) First Five Year Plan (1928–1932) concentrated on the development of industry, power supply and transport.

(iii) Second Five Year Plan (1933–1938) concentrated on transport — water, road and rail. It also built on the developments of the first Five Year Plan.

(iv) Third Five Year Plan (1938–1941). This should have concentrated on consumer goods. However, a greater emphasis was given to defence spending due to the international situation. The plan ended with the German invasion of Russia in June 1941.

(c) Results

(i) The Five Year Plans saw improvements in heavy industry. The output of coal, steel, oil and electricity increased.

(ii) Improvements were also made in transport. Publicity was given to achievements such as the construction of the Belomor-Baltic Canal. However, this was not deep enough for many of the Red Navy's larger ships and therefore its value was exaggerated.

(iii) The output of tractors increased. This was very important for the future of agriculture.

(iv) New towns and industrial sites, such as Sverdlovsk and Magnitogorsk, were developed.

(v) Hydro-electric power was introduced. The Dnieper Dam was constructed to help provide this power. It was Europe's largest dam.

(vi) Working conditions were very poor.

    (a) Work books were reintroduced. Workers were told where to work.

    (b) Food was in short supply.

    (c) Discipline was strict. Absenteeism became grounds for instant dismissal after 1932. Absenteeism meant being as little as 20 minutes late for work. Stealing state property became a capital offence in August 1932.

    (d) Wages increased although there were little consumer goods available to buy.

(vii) Incentives were offered to workers meeting targets — better housing and pay for instance. The Stakhanovite movement was set up to publicise the achievements of workers. This was named after a miner, Alexei Stakhanov, who cut fourteen times the normal amount of coal in one shift. He did have the help of unskilled auxiliaries.

(viii) The numbers of doctors and nurses rose, as did people involved in education. A campaign was begun to improve literacy within the USSR. Special emphasis was placed on technical education, which would produce the engineers and skilled workers required for industry.

Overall the industrialisation campaign can be considered a success. By 1940, the Soviet Union was one of the leading industrial powers, only Germany and the USA were stronger. More importantly, the advances made in the thirties gave the USSR the industrial strength to repulse the German invasion of June 1941. However, it was completed at a terrible cost to the workers, thousands died during the construction programme.

14

Activities of the Communist Government under Stalin as Demonstrated by Collectivisation

Reasons for Introducing Collectivisaton

(a) Russian agriculture was backward and inefficient. The NEP was not producing enough surplus grain. In 1928, Stalin claimed there was a threat of famine.

(b) Stalin hoped that if agriculture could be made efficient then

    (i) the workers would be fed,

    (ii) surplus grain could be sold abroad to raise money. This, in turn, could be used to buy machinery.

(c) NEP allowed private trade. It allowed the existence of Kulaks (rich or well-off peasant farmers). Communism was opposed to this on ideological grounds. Collectivisation would destroy the differences between the peasantry.

(d) The state controlled only 3% of the agricultural land. The rest belonged to the peasantry. By collectivising the land, the Communist Government would make it easier to control. Rather than dealing with several million families, the Communists would have to deal with a few thousand collective farms.

(e) One of the reasons War Communism was abandoned was the attitude of the peasantry. They had refused to hand over their grain to the Government without a fight. Stalin was determined that this would not happen again.

Organisation of Collectivisation

(a) Several farms were grouped together to form a collective. All the land and labour were pooled. All the members of the collective worked for the common good.

(b) Ninety per cent of the produce was sold to the state.

(c) The state made equipment, such as tractors, available. Motor Tractor Stations were set up to supply tractors to several collectives. New methods of farming were also introduced.

(d) Peasants made a living from a share of the profits of the collective. If they worked on a state farm they were given a fixed wage. They were allowed to keep their own vegetable plot which they could either sell or use themselves.

Stalin and the Kulaks

(a) At first, Stalin tried to persuade peasants to join the collectives by offering incentives such as free housing and hospitals. This failed and force had to be used.

(b) Peasants slaughtered their livestock and destroyed their grain rather than hand them over to the collectives.

(c) Agricultural production in Russia, 1928 and 1934.

	1928	1934
Grain (m. tons)	73·3	67·6
Cattle (m. head)	70·5	42·4
Pigs (m. head)	26·0	22·6
Sheep and goats (m. head)	146·7	51·9

The figures show that Collectivisation was a disaster for the Soviet Union. It resulted in a famine in 1931–1932.

(d) The Kulaks refused to enter the collectives. Stalin destroyed them by

(i) Using the jealousy of the poor peasants. They attacked the Kulaks and seized their property.

(ii) Using the secret police to arrest them. Kulaks were either deported to remote areas, such as Siberia, or executed. Many were sent to the Gulags (labour camps).

Dekulakisation destroyed the most effective farmers in Russian agriculture.

(e) Figures vary as to the numbers of peasants who died during collectivisation. Estimates range from 5–7 million. Many deaths occurred in the famine because Stalin refused to help the peasants.

(f) Stalin's second wife, Nadezhda Alliluyeva, was horrified by the effects of collectivisation. She is rumoured to have committed suicide after an argument with Stalin over his treatment of the peasants.

(g) By 1941, 98% of peasant holdings were collectivised.
By 1939, Soviet agricultural productivity had returned to the level recorded for Tsarist Russia in 1913.

15

Activities of the Communist Government under Stalin
as Demonstrated by Political Purges

Political Purges

(a) This refers to the period from around 1934 until 1938. Stalin decided to destroy all potential forms of opposition to his rule within the USSR.

(b) Stalin wanted to terrify the population into obeying him without questioin. This led to the start of the 'terror'.

(c) Many people seized the opportunity to settle old scores. Many others denounced their friends as traitors because they were afraid they might be regarded as disloyal.

The Kirov Murder

(a) In December 1934, Sergei Kirov, the popular leader of the Communist party in Leningrad, was murdered. He was seen as a real rival to Stalin as leader of the Soviet Union. Many suspect that Stalin had organised the murder of Kirov. This incident was used as the reason for the NKVD (the secret police) to arrest opponents of Stalin.

(b) Russians executed or imprisoned 1934–1939.

Two-thirds of the members of the original Bolshevik Government.
One-third of Red Army officers.
Ninety-eight members of the Central Committee of the Communist Party. This included important figures such as Zinoviev, Kamenev and Bukharin.
One-third of the Communist Party membership.
Seven million Kulaks, factory workers, intellectuals.

In all, around ten million people were killed during this period.

(c) Many people were sent to the labour camps (Gulags), which were controlled by the NKVD. They formed a very important source of labour for the industrialisation campaign.

(d) Show trials were organised in which the defendants usually confessed to false charges. They did this possibly because they were tortured or threats made to their family. Certainly this appears to have been the case with Bukharin. After being found guilty, the defendants were usually shot. In 1938 alone, the NKVD shot 350 000 people.

Results

(a) Stalin was the undisputed leader of the Soviet Union.

(b) People obeyed Stalin without question.

(c) The Soviet Union lost many of its best army officers. This caused many problems during the German invasion of 1941.

By 1941, the Soviet Union was controlled by Stalin and his secret police, the NKVD. The Republic was portrayed as the most democratic in the world.

The 1936 Constitution was set up by Stalin to prove that this was the case. It allowed

(a) All people over 18 to vote for people to sit in the Supreme Soviet.

(b) The Supreme Soviet chose people to sit in the Presidium.

(c) The Presidium chose the Council of Ministers.

(d) The Council of Ministers chose a Premier.

However, this was not the most democratic constitution in the world because

(a) There was no choice of party. Only the Communists were allowed to exist.

(b) Stalin chose the people who were on the electoral lists.

As a result, Stalin controlled the Soviet Union until his death in 1953.

UNIT 3 — People and Power

CONTEXT D: Germany 1918–1939

1

The Effects on Germany of the end of the First World War and the Peace Settlement

Condition of Germany at the end of the war

By November 1918, the German people were suffering severe hardships.

  (i) The fall in agricultural production caused by the large numbers of men fighting in the war led to food shortages.

 (ii) Industry and agriculture were geared up to producing supplies for the war effort. The people in the towns suffered severe shortages of food and fuel.

(iii) The allied blockade meant that goods were not reaching Germany's ports.

(iv) The Spanish influenza epidemic which swept through Germany in the summer of 1918 had killed 400 000 German civilians.

 (v) German casualties at the front increased due to the Spring Offensive launched by Germany's generals in March 1918.

The Fall of the Kaiser

Kaiser Wilhelm II abdicated on November 9th 1918, on the advice of his generals. He fled to Holland.

The main reasons for the Kaiser's abdication were:

  (i) He and the rest of the royal family had become deeply unpopular with the German people. They blamed the Kaiser for the hardships they were suffering.

118

(ii) The Kaiser's Government was losing control of the country. Workers and Soldiers Councils were being set up to take control of the towns and cities.

(iii) The Kaiser's generals warned him that morale in the armed forces was dangerously low and that defeat was inevitable. Germany's allies (Austria, Hungary, Turkey and Bulgaria) had already pulled out of the war.

(iv) President Wilson of the USA said that no armistice would be possible whilst the Kaiser remained on his throne.

The Peace Settlement

The German people expected a fair peace based on the ideas of President Wilson. The US President had come to Europe in 1919, promising a just and fair settlement.

The announcement of the terms of the Treaty of Versailles led to great bitterness in Germany.

(i) *The Diktat* — Germany had no say in the terms of the treaty but was ordered to sign within two weeks or their country would be invaded. Germans referred to the treaty as the 'diktat': the dictated peace. They did not see why they should be bound by such a treaty when they had been forced to sign.

(ii) *The War Guilt Clause* — Clause 231 of the treaty forced Germany to accept total blame for starting the war. Germans felt this was unfair because Germany had not been the first or the only country to declare war. Other Germans were bitter because the new Germany was being held responsible for the actions of the Kaiser's Government, which had now been removed.

(iii) *Reparations* — As a consequence of the War Guilt Clause, the Germans were forced to pay for the cost of repairing the damage that had been done. Most Germans resented this great burden on their economy, which had already been severely weakened by war.

(iv) *Loss of territory*

Germany lost: 13·5% of her territory
12·5% of her population
15% of her agriculture
16% of her coal producing areas
48% of her iron producing areas.

These terms were resented because the loss of important industrial areas would make Germany's economic recovery even more difficult. The loss of territory on Germany's eastern frontiers was particularly resented because many Germans were placed under Polish rule. Part of Germany (East Prussia) was separated from the rest of the country by the Polish corridor.

(v) *Loss of colonies* — All Germany's African and Asian colonies were confiscated and eventually given to Britain and France. The resulting loss of trade and raw materials was seen by Germans as another obstacle to German recovery.

(vi) *Ban on Anschluss* — The ban on union between Germany and the new German-speaking state of Austria was seen as unnecessarily harsh and unfair. Separating two German-speaking peoples at a time when other nationalities, like the Poles, were being united in one nation was seen as unjust.

(vii) *Disarmament* — The reduction of the German army to 100 000 men and the destruction of the navy and airforce was seen as further unnecessary humiliation of a once great power.

Opposition to the Treaty of Versailles

The Peace Settlement became a cause of great discontent. The new republic became associated in the minds of many Germans with national disgrace and humiliation. Nationalists claimed that Germany had been betrayed by its new leaders.

The Stab in the Back Myth

At this time, the myth arose that the German army had not been defeated on the field of battle but had been stabbed in the back by the Socialist politicians who had taken power in November 1918. According to this view, the disgrace of Versailles could have been avoided.

The Formation and Characteristics of the Weimar Republic

Formation of the new German Republic

By November 1918, it looked as though Germany was about to undergo a revolution similar to the Communist revolution that had happened in Russia a year earlier.

(i) Feeling against the country's rulers was running high. There were strong demands for the removal of the Kaiser and withdrawal from the war.

(ii) Sailors at Kiel naval base mutinied in response to an order to attack the Royal Navy. The mutiny spread to other ports.

(iii) Workers and Soldiers Councils were taking over the running of Germany's towns and cities.

On November 9th, the German Socialist Scheidemann declared that Germany had become a republic. The Kaiser's last chancellor, Prince Max of Baden, resigned. He was replaced by the leader of the SPD (Social Democrats), Frederich Ebert.

Ebert announced the formation of a provisional government which would rule Germany until elections could be held.

Characteristics of the Republic

Republic

Ebert announced that Wilhelm II would be the last Kaiser of Germany. No royal families would now be permitted.

Democratic

Although Ebert had not gained power democratically, i.e. through an election, he promised that Germany would be given a democratic constitution. The people of Germany would be given the right to elect their own leaders.

The Weimar Constitution

In August 1919, a new constitution was adopted by the new German republic. At that time, the Government had moved to escape the violence and chaos of Berlin and was meeting in the town of Weimar in eastern Germany. Under the new Weimar Constitution, Germany adopted a new political system.

The Weimar Constitution soon presented problems which resulted in discontent among many Germans.

(i) *The Reichstag* — The new parliament of Germany was to be elected by all men and women over the age of 20 by the system of proportional representation: which meant that for every 60 000 votes a party received, it got one seat in the Reichstag. Elections had to be held every four years.

The Government had to have the support of at least 50% of the deputies in the Reichstag. The leader of the Government was known as the Chancellor.

Problem:

Proportional representation meant that many small parties were able to gain seats in the Reichstag. No one party was ever able to gain the 50% of the votes necessary to form a government. This led to a series of weak coalition governments formed by groups of parties. Disagreements among these parties often led the coalition to collapse, which meant another election was required. The average time that a government lasted during the Weimar republic was ten months. Germans never got to know, let alone trust, their leaders.

(ii) *The Reichsrat* — Each of the regions (lander) of Germany had traditionally had its own parliament and government. These regional parliaments remained, but their powers were reduced. Each regional parliament sent a representative to the Reichsrat in Berlin. This parliament had limited powers to change laws made by the Reichstag.

Problem:

Many Germans resented the centralisation of power which occurred under the constitution. Regions with a strong sense of identity disliked being ruled from Berlin.

(iii) *The President* — To replace the Kaiser as head of state, a President was to be elected by the people once every seven years. Although he had little say in the day to day running of the country, he could step in if there was a crisis and rule Germany by himself. The President was Commander-in-Chief of the armed forces and had the power to appoint or remove the Chancellor.

Problem:

The constitution meant that in certain circumstances the President could exert tremendous influence over the running of the country. Germans were concerned about one man having so much power.

Conclusion

The Weimar Constitution caused discontent among many Germans. The constant elections and changes of coalition governments left many people feeling that Germany had no strong leadership during times of national crisis. The centralisation of power in Berlin was resented by the individual states. In the eyes of many Germans, the President did not command the same respect as the charismatic Hohenzollern royal family had. Ebert, the first President, became an object of ridicule for some Germans.

Other aspects of the constitution caused discontent. The new rights of citizenship given to Jews were resented by some Germans. The replacement of the old German red, white and black flag with a new red, black and gold tricolour led to protests by nationalist groups.

Attempts to secure political freedoms and the rights of the individual under the Weimar Constitution.

Background — Rights and freedoms had been strictly limited in the Kaiser's Germany. The SPD had suffered greatly under this regime. The democratic parties which took power after the election of January 1919 were determined that the constitution of the new republic would increase the rights and freedoms of the individual.

Political freedoms

(i) All men and women over 20 were entitled to vote in local and national elections.

(ii) All Germans were entitled to belong to the political party of their choice.

Rights of the Individual

(i) *Freedom of Speech* — All Germans had the right to express opinions freely and openly.

(ii) *Freedom of Association* — All Germans had the right to organise and attend peaceful meetings.

(iii) *Freedom of the Press* — Newspapers were allowed to operate without interference or censorship by the Government.

(iv) *Freedom of Worship* — All Germans had the right to worship under the religion of their choice without fear of persecution.

(v) *Rights of Privacy* — A person's home was to be a place of safety. The authorities were not allowed to breech this privacy without good reason.

(vi) *Freedom from Arrest Without Trial* — No person could be held against his will by the authorities without the benefit of a fair trial.

3

Attempts to Overthrow the German Republic as seen in the Spartacist Revolt of 1919 and the Beer Hall Putsch of 1923

The Spartacist Revolt

The Spartacists were a group of revolutionaries who had been heavily involved in the events leading to the Kaiser's abdication in November 1918. They had helped to spread the revolt following the Kiel Mutiny and had been prominent in the Workers and Soldiers Councils which appeared in most German cities.

Demands of the Spartacists

The Spartacists, led by Rosa Luxemburg and Karl Liebknecht, had become disillusioned with the policies of Ebert's moderate socialist government. They demanded:

(i) Abandonment of plans for democratic elections.

(ii) More power to the Workers and Soldiers Councils.

(iii) Removal of the powers of the German army, civil service and judiciary.

(iv) Industry and agriculture to be taken over by the workers.

The Ebert-Groener Pact

On November 9th 1918, General Groener, senior commander in the German army, contacted Ebert, the new leader of Germany. In a secret telephone conversation, Ebert promised not to interfere in the running of the army. In return, Groener promised the loyalty of the army to the new Government. This deal was to assume great importance during the Spartacist Rising.

The Spartacist Rising

The Spartacist Rising was an attempted revolution against the new Government of Germany. The main events were

(i) Spartacists demonstrations against Ebert's government in Berlin in December 1918. Ebert ordered soldiers to disperse the demonstrators. Shots were fired and 16 protesters were killed.

(ii) *December 23rd 1918* — Spartacists, supported by sailors, broke into the chancellory building and arrested Ebert at gunpoint. He was released when he promised to give concessions to the Spartacists.

(iii) *December 31st 1918* — Spartacist leaders lost patience with Ebert and called for a Communist revolution in Germany.

(iv) *Bloody Week (January 6th to 13th 1919)* — Spartacist demonstrators took to the streets in an armed uprising against the Government. They were reinforced by Freikorps. These were bands of ex-servicemen who were bitterly opposed to Communism. Ebert's Defence Minister, Gustav Noske, organised the Freikorps units. They played a major part in crushing the Spartacists in bloody street battles. Spartacist leaders were executed.

Extreme left wing resistance to the new republic had been crushed.

The Beerhall Putsch, 1923

By November 1923, there was much discontent in Bavaria, the main state in southern Germany. Adolf Hitler came to prominence at this time as leader of the NSDAP, an extreme nationalist group which was deeply opposed to the Weimar Republic.

Reasons for discontent in Bavaria

    (i) Many Bavarians resented the fact that they had less control over their own affairs under the Weimar Constitution. Under the Kaiser, Bavaria had its own royal family and greater independence.

    (ii) The French invasion of the Ruhr in January 1923 and the hyper-inflation which followed led to an increase in discontent with the Government in Berlin.

    (iii) Nationalists in Bavaria were outraged that in November 1923 the new Government, under Stresemann, appeared to be giving in to the French by calling off German resistance in the Ruhr and agreeing to pay reparations.

The Plan

    (i) Hitler planned to seize control of the Bavarian Government.

    (ii) A 'March on Berlin' would then take place. Hitler wanted to emulate the Italian Fascist leader, Mussolini, who had taken power after the March on Rome by his Italian Fascists in 1922. Hitler expected a great spontaneous rising against the Weimar Republic.

    (iii) Hitler planned a national revolution which would bring him to power in Germany.

The main events of the Beerhall Putsch Revolt were

    (i) On the evening of November 8th, 3000 people gathered in the Burgerbraukellar in Munich to hear the leader of the Bavarian Government, Von Kahr, speak against the Weimar Government in Berlin. The meeting was attended by other Bavarian leaders: Von Seisser (head of Bavarian police) and Lossow (chief of the army in Bavaria).

    These leaders had already shown resistance to the German Government by refusing to carry out instructions given in Berlin.

    (ii) Adolf Hitler, with 600 supporters including Field Marshall Ludendorff the famous First World War leader, burst into the meeting. Hitler announced that he intended to lead a 'national revolution'. He received much support from the drinkers in the hall and was able to persuade the Bavarian leaders present to support the plan.

(iii) On November 9th, the Bavarian leaders withdrew their support for Hitler's bold plan. The Bavarian police and army were ordered to crush the putsch.

(iv) Hitler and Ludendorf led a march into Munich, where they were confronted by Bavarian troops who opened fire to disperse the marchers. Sixteen were killed. Hitler and Ludendorf were arrested.

(v) Hitler was tried for treason. In his defence he made a speech against the Weimar Republic. He claimed that he had acted as a patriot and dismissed the charge of treason against a Government which had betrayed Germany in November 1918. Hitler was given a five year prison sentence with parole after 18 months. Ludendorf was set free.

On his release from jail, Hitler gave the NSDAP a new direction. Resistance to the Weimar Republic would now be organised using legal methods rather than through violent revolutionary methods.

4

Economic Problems of the Weimar Republic, 1919–1933

1920–1921 — Erzberger Reforms

The main economic problem facing the Weimar Republic in its early years was inflation. In the early 1920s, Finance Minister Matthias Erzberger attempted to tackle the growing inflation in Germany by taking steps to reduce Government spending and increase taxation on the well off. Erzberger was forced to abandon these policies because of strong opposition. The Finance Minister was eventually forced to resign.

1923 Hyper-inflation

By November 1923, inflation had destroyed the value of the German mark.

The value of the mark collapsed.

July	1914	£1	=	20 marks
Jan.	1919	£1	=	35 marks
Jan.	1920	£1	=	256 marks

Jan.	1922	£1	=	764 marks
Jan.	1923	£1	=	71 888 marks
July	1923	£1	=	1 413 648 marks
Sept.	1923	£1	=	3 954 408 000 marks
Nov.	1923	£1	=	1 680 800 000 000 000 marks

Causes of the Hyper-inflation

(i) The First World War — left Germany deeply in debt. The Government had taken to printing money to cover its spending. This led to inflation.

(ii) The Treaty of Versailles — Losses suffered by Germany hindered economic recovery.

(iii) French Invasion of the Ruhr — January 1923. The French took over Germany's main industrial area in order to seize reparations. The German Government supported passive resistance by German workers in the Ruhr. This meant that the Government had to pay workers for producing nothing. They did this by printing more money.

Economic Effects of the Hyper-inflation.

(i) Trade with other countries became impossible.

(ii) Businesses could not cope with the problems caused by the inflation. They closed down and workers were laid off.

(iii) Prices rose ahead of wages.

Social Effects of Hyper-inflation

Some people could cope better than others with the soaring prices. Millions, whose incomes could not keep up with price rises, faced starvation.

Cost of one loaf of bread in Berlin in marks

1914	0·35
1918	0·63
1922	163
1923 (Jan)	250
1923 (July)	3 465
1923 (Sept)	1 500 000
1923 (Nov)	201 000 000 000

Working Class

Wage earners suffered a fall in their living standards. A typical factory worker faced a 30% cut in real wages. However, wage earners were not as badly hit as other groups.

Reasons:

(i) Employers paid wages daily, in some cases twice daily.

(ii) Factory workers were sometimes paid with goods instead of cash. They could barter these goods to get the things they needed.

(iii) Some employers introduced a voucher system instead of paying wages in cash. The vouchers could be exchanged for the factory's products. Workers could use these vouchers to trade for things they needed.

Middle Class

People who were paid a monthly salary suffered badly because their pay was unable to keep up with daily price rises. Savers found that their investments were ruined by the inflation.

Upper Middle Class

Property owners whose income came from rents were often badly affected. Rent increases were tightly controlled by law and did not rise in step with inflation. Some shrewd businessmen, however, did well out of the inflation by paying off debts in worthless currency or by speculating on the currency markets.

The Old and Unemployed

People who relied on state benefits found that these payments did not keep up with inflation. These people faced severe hardship.

Conclusion

The hyper-inflation led to great discontent, especially among middle class people. The effect of inflation on their salaries and savings was disastrous. Many such people were reduced to poverty. Many middle class people never forgot the humiliation they suffered and lost what faith they had in the new Weimar Republic.

1924–1929 The Period of Stability

The period during which Germany was under the influence of the shrewd and skilful politician Gustav Stresemann was one of relative prosperity.

Stresemann's policies, first as Chancellor and then as Foreign Minister, seemed to bring about a period of stability. In 1927, German industrial production exceeded 1913 levels. However, there were still problems beneath the surface. Stresemann himself said that at this time Germany was "dancing on a volcano". By this he meant that if the loans were withdrawn the prosperity would end.

The main underlying weaknesses were:

(i) *Loans*

Germany received 25 000 million marks in foreign loans during this period. Most of the money came from the USA.

These loans were short term. The money had to be repaid, or the loan renewed after a short period, usually around 90 days. In normal circumstances, US financiers were happy to renew the loans.

(ii) *Reparations*

Although the Dawes Plan, which Stresemann negotiated in 1924, scaled down Germany's payments by extending the repayment period until 1983, the burden of debt remained.

In 1929, the Young Plan extended the repayment period even further but the total debt remained the same.

(iii) *Agriculture*

Farmers did not share in the period of prosperity. A world wide fall in agricultural prices meant that it was particularly difficult for small farmers to make a living. Many fell into debt and faced eviction.

(iv) *Unemployment*

Unemployment fell steadily between 1924 and 1927. However, many businesses soon found that they were producing more than they could sell. They began to lay off workers. Unemployment in Germany was starting to rise even before the Wall Street Crash took place.

1929–1934 — The Depression

The Wall Street Crash and the international financial crisis which followed had a devastating effect on Germany.

Causes of Depression in Germany

(i) *Wall Street Crash* — The collapse of share prices on the US Stock Exchange meant that US investors faced ruin. They responded by recalling loans that they had made outside America. This created a financial crisis across the world.

(ii) The brief period of economic stability in Germany, between 1924 and 1929, had been funded largely by US loans. When US financiers recalled their loans, banks and businesses collapsed and millions of people were made unemployed.

Effects of the Depression on Germany

(i) There was a dramatic rise in unemployment in Germany.

Unemployment in Germany

1928	650 000
1929	1 320 000
1930	3 000 000
1931	4 350 000
1932	5 102 000
1933	6 100 000

(ii) Soon after the Wall Street Crash, disagreements over how best to deal with the crisis led to the fall of the 'Grand Coalition'. This moderate coalition had governed Germany throughout the period of prosperity.

(iii) The new Government, under Chancellor Bruning, took urgent measures to restore the economy by cutting government spending. Wages for government employees were reduced, unemployment benefit was cut. These deflationary measures were accompanied by increases in taxation. Government economic policies had a bad effect on the living standards of many people.

(iv) The economic collapse had severe political repercussions. Political parties with new and radical solutions to Germany's problems became popular.

% Vote for extremist parties in Reichstag elections

	1924	1928	1930	July 1932
KPD	9	10·6	14·3	14·6
Nazis	3	2·6	18·3	37·4

5

Discontent against the Weimar Republic and the coming to power of the National Socialists in 1933–1934

Discontent against the Weimar Republic

Discontent in Germany reached a peak in March 1933. Many groups had reasons to be disillusioned with the Weimar Republic.

(i) *Unemployed*

Unemployment exceeded six million in January 1933. The Government had cut benefits to the unemployed and seemed unable to tackle the crisis.

(ii) *Farmers*

The agricultural slump of the 1920s had taken its toll among small farmers in the west and north of Germany. There was much bitterness towards the governments of the Weimar era which had done little to ease the farmers' problems.

(iii) *Middle Classes*

Many middle class people believed that not enough had been done to control the growth of Communism in Germany. Many property owners also remembered the suffering inflicted on them by the hyper-inflation and did not trust the Government to deal effectively with economic problems. Many such people were looking for stronger leadership for Germany than the democratic Weimar Constitution had provided.

(iv) *Youth*

Many young people were disillusioned by the succession of elderly politicians who had led the country during the years of the Weimar Republic. They were looking for stronger, more vigorous leadership.

(v) *Nationalists*

German nationalists still associated the Weimar Republic with the shameful defeat of 1918 and acceptance of the hated Versailles settlement. Nationalists united to campaign against the adoption of the Young Plan, under which the German Government agreed to continue making reparations payments. To nationalists, this was a further humiliation for Germany.

The Coming to Power of the National Socialists 1933–1934

Steps to Hitler becoming Chancellor:

September 1930 — NSDAP first election success

In Reichstag elections, the NSDAP gained 18·3% of the vote. They became the second largest party with 107 seats.

Hitler refused to go into coalition with any other party so no government could be formed which had the support of the Reichstag.

President Hindenburg appointed, as Chancellor, Von Bruning of the Centre Party. He governed Germany making use of Hindenburg's emergency powers.

March 1932 — Presidential elections

Presidential Elections. Hitler stood for President but was defeated by Hindenburg.

Hindenburg	19 359 000
Hitler	13 418 000
Thalman (KPD)	3 706 000

July 1932 — NSDAP became largest party

NSDAP won 37·4% of the vote and gained 230 seats in the Reichstag elections. This made them the largest party in the Reichstag.

With no coalition possible, Hindenburg made his friend, Von Papen, Chancellor.

November 1932 — Fall of Von Papen Government

Von Papen had little support in the Reichstag or in Germany. Hindenburg removed him and called new elections.

NSDAP lost some support but remained the largest party with 196 seats (33·1% of the vote).

Hindenburg decided to appoint General Von Schleicher as Chancellor.

January 1933 — Fall of Von Schleicher Government — Hitler becomes Chancellor

Von Schleicher proved to be as unpopular as Von Papen. Hindenburg was persuaded by a group of conservative politicians (army generals and landowners) that the only way to solve the crisis and to bring about an acceptable government which would have popular support was to make Hitler Chancellor at the head of a conservative government. Von Papen was made Vice-Chancellor. He assured Hindenburg that Hitler could be controlled.

Hitler's first action was to call new elections.

Steps to Hitler becoming Fuhrer

February 1933 (The Reichstag Fire)

On the night of 27th February, six days before elections were to be held, there was a fire in the Reichstag building.

Hitler claimed that the fire was a signal for the start of a communist revolution. Next day he asked Hindenburg for an Emergency Decree to deal with the crisis. Hitler was empowered to lock up his communist and socialist opponents.

These scare tactics persuaded many Germans to vote for Hitler.

March 1933 — The Enabling Act — Power of Reichstag destroyed

NSDAP gained 44% of the vote and 288 seats. An agreement with the DNVP allowed Hitler to form a National Socialist Government.

On March 23rd, Hitler passed an Enabling Act. This amendment to the Weimar Constitution allowed Hitler to rule without having to consult the Reichstag for a period of four years. Under this law, all other political parties were banned.

April 1933 — Power of local government destroyed

Hitler abolished the lander parliaments and local government in Germany. Instead, a network of officials was organised to carry out Hitler's orders and keep every citizen under control.

May 1933 — Power of opposition parties destroyed

Stormtroopers attack SPD and KPD headquarters and arrest party officials.

November 1933

Reichstag elections were held. Only NSDAP candidates could stand in the election. After this election, the Reichstag only met to hear speeches by Hitler. The Reichstag had no power.

May 1934 — Independence of legal system destroyed

The People's Court was established. It tried 'enemies of the state' for treason. Its proceedings were kept secret.

June 1934 — The Night of the Long Knives

Hitler ordered a purge of opposition within the NSDAP. The Stormtroopers (SA) were the main target. Its leaders had become both a threat and an embarrassment to Hitler.

Various other opponents were arrested and imprisoned or executed during this reign of terror.

August 1934 — Death of Hindenburg

The last major obstacle to Hitler's dictatorship was removed when President Hindenburg died at the age of 87.

Hitler joined the positions of Chancellor and President and made himself 'Fuehrer and Reich Chancellor'. The German army swore an oath of personal loyalty to Hitler.

Conclusion

The main reasons for the coming to power of the National Socialists were:

(i) *Economic Crisis*

The despair caused by the depression led to a collapse in support for moderate, democratic parties and the rise of extremism.

(ii) *Collapse of Democracy*

The rise of extremist parties meant that no coalition government was possible. Power passed to President Hindenburg who finally allowed himself to be convinced that the only solution to the crisis in Germany was to make Hitler Chancellor.

(iii) *Fear of Communism*

The rise of the KPD led many Germans to see Hitler as the only alternative to Communism.

(iv) *The Appeal of National Socialism*

Through the skilful use of propaganda, the National Socialists convinced Germans that only Hitler could bring strong leadership and national revival.

(v) *Ineffectiveness of Opposition*

Through violent intimidation and cunning, Hitler was able to outwit and destroy his opponents.

6

Formation and Characteristics of the National Socialist Government

(i) *The End of Democratic Government*

On March 23rd 1933, Hitler passed the Enabling Act which allowed him to rule Germany without consulting the Reichstag. Hitler could pass laws as and when he saw fit.

(ii) *The Fuehrer Principle*

Germany was now to be governed under the 'Fuehrer Principle' whereby one man, the Fuehrer (leader), had ultimate power.

(iii) *The One Party State*

Parties which had opposed the Nazis were banned.

KPD banned 26th May 1933.,
SPD banned 22nd June 1933.

On 14th July 1933, Hitler passed the 'Law against the Formation of New Parties' which stated that the National Socialist Party was the only party which was allowed to exist.

(iv) *The Police State*

The Secret State Police (Gestapo) was ordered to root out all possible opposition to Hitler's rule. Suspects could be arrested and imprisoned without trial. Concentration camps were built for 'enemies of the Reich', e.g. Jews, socialists and pacifists, etc.

The rights and freedoms laid down by the Weimar Constitution were removed. There was no longer freedom of speech, the Gestapo used a network of informers to catch those who said anything against the Reich. The Gestapo could enter anyone's property without restriction.

7

National Socialism in Power:
Treatment of the Jews, Youth Movements and Education, Intimidation, Militarism.

Treatment of the Jews

National Socialist Ideology

(i) The Jews were an inferior race of people. They lacked the virtues of other superior races, especially the Aryan race, to which the 'true Germans' belonged.

(ii) The presence of the Jews in Germany and the resultant 'inbreeding' between the races had led to a corrupting of the superior Aryan race. The Jews were a threat to racial purity in Germany.

(iii) There was an international Jewish conspiracy against other races. Through their control in international communism and international capitalism, the Jews were attempting to gain control of the world.

Government Action Against the Jews

(i) *April 1st 1933* — SA organises a boycott of all Jewish businesses.

(ii) *May 1935* — Jews forbidden to join the German army.

(iii) *Summer of 1935* — Signs appear in shops and restaurants "Jews not wanted here".

(iv) *September 15th 1935 — The Nuremburg Laws*

Reich Citizenship Law — Jews banned from being German citizens — not allowed to vote or work for the Government.

Law for the Protection of German Blood and Honour. Marriage and sexual relations between Jews and Germans were forbidden.

(v) *October 5th 1938* — Jews forced to have their passports stamped with the letter 'J'.

(vi) *November 9th 1938 — 'Kristalnacht' (Night of Broken Glass).*

Following the assassination of a National Socialist Official by a Jew, widespread attacks were made on synagogues and other Jewish property.

(vii) *November 15th 1938* — Jews banned from attending German schools.

Conclusion

The actions of the Government against the Jews clearly reflected National Socialist ideology. As a result of his racialist views, Hitler wanted Jews to be isolated from Germans. This policy continued after 1939 with the establishment of Jewish ghettos and the 'Final Solution': the plan to wipe out the Jews in Europe.

Youth Movements and Education

National Socialist Ideology

(i) Children were vital to the future of Germany. National Socialist propaganda, in the years before Hitler came to power, stressed the importance of the young in leading Germany into a new age. They would become the new 'Master Race' which would dominate Europe.

(ii) It was vital that young people should be indoctrinated with National Socialist beliefs and values, such as putting the interests of the State above self interest.

(iii) Boys should be given military training to prepare them for the struggles which lay ahead of Germany.

(iv) Girls must be prepared to bring up the new racially pure master race.

Hitler Youth

The main characteristics of Hitler Youth movements were:

(i) There were separate organisations and activities for boys and girls.

(ii) Indoctrination in National Socialist beliefs and values was an aim of all Hitler Youth organisations.

(iii) Jews and other non-Germans were banned from Hitler Youth organisations.

(iv) There was intimidation of young Germans who did not join the youth movements. Parents could be imprisoned for refusing to allow their children to join youth organisations.

Education

The main changes in education were:

(i) All teachers had to belong to the National Socialist Teachers' League.

(ii) New textbooks were introduced which introduced National Socialist ideology into most school subjects. For example, history books focussed on the history of the NSDAP and victories from Germany's past.

(iii) New subjects were introduced like 'political education' and 'racial hygiene'.

(iv) Jewish children were at first singled out for ridicule and eventually banned from attending German schools (1938).

Conclusion

Government policy on education clearly reflected National Socialist ideology. The reorganisation of education was one of Hitler's main priorities. Children in Germany were indoctrinated with National Socialist ideology at school and after school in their Hitler Youth meetings.

Intimidation

The National Socialists made systematic use of threats to deter opposition.

Methods of intimidation used by the National Socialists:

(i) *Speeches* — National Socialist leaders made it clear that they were intolerant of any opposition and their determination to crush enemies of the state.

(ii) *Propaganda* — Josef Goebbels was skilled at including an underlying threat of menace in National Socialist posters, newspapers and films, e.g. the violent death of the Jewish anti-hero in the film *Jude Suss*.

(iii) *Paramilitary organisations* — The common presence of uniformed SA and SS on the streets.

(iv) *Marches and Rallies* — At National Socialist events there was always a show of force by uniformed SS and SA.

(v) *The Police State* — The sinister presence of the Gestapo backed by a network of informants.

Conclusion

The right of the State to protect itself by any means possible — including the systematic use of threats — was an essential aspect of National Socialist ideology.

Militarism

According to National Socialist ideology, military ideas were vital to the revival of Germany.

(i) *Leadership* — It was essential that Germany should have a strong leader to make all the decisions.

(ii) *Common interest over self-interest* — No German should put his own interests above those of Germany. Self-sacrifice in the interests of the State was seen as a great virtue.

(iii) *Discipline, loyalty and obedience* — All Germans should learn to trust and obey the Fuehrer without question.

(iv) *Uniformity* — According to National Socialist ideology, individuals do not matter and it was wrong to stand out from the crowd.

(v) *Struggle* — Nazi ideology was based on the idea of struggle; the struggle to make Germany great again and to secure the future of the 'master race'.

Militarism in Germany under the National Socialist Government

(i) Organisations were set up for most groups in German society. For example, the National Socialist Teacher's League, Hitler Youth organisations, the German Labour Front. Each organisation had its own military style, uniforms and insignia.

(ii) Festivals and rallies were held regularly where marches, military music and uniforms predominated.

(iii) A great party rally was held each year at Nuremburg. A special stadium was designed to hold over 100 000 people. Hitler made a speech before ranks of uniformed party members. The event was broadcast on radio and films were made for the cinema.

(iv) Hitler ordered a massive rearmament programme and, after 1935, the size of the German army was increased. Conscription was also introduced. The new armed forces were displayed to the German people and to the outside world in great parades and displays.

Conclusion

The importance of militarism in National Socialist ideology was clearly shown in the actions of Hitler's Government. Life in Germany became a succession of parades and rallies. All Germans were expected to conform to the military ideals of discipline, obedience and loyalty to the Fuehrer. Hitler soon placed Germany's armed forces on a war footing and the people were expected to applaud the successes of his armed forces abroad. People who spoke for peace were regarded as criminals. People suspected of pacifism were sent to concentration camps.

8

Opposition to National Socialism by Socialists, Communists and the Churches

Socialist and Communist Opposition

Before Hitler came to power, the Socialists and Communists had been his bitterest enemies.

Nature of Socialist/Communist opposition before 1933

(i) SPD and KPD propaganda portrayed the NSDAP as an anti-democratic, anti-working class party in the pockets of big business and landowners.

(ii) Left wing paramilitary organisations — the Reichsbanner and the Red Front — fought the NSDAP Stormtroopers on the street.

(iii) SPD and KPD campaigned strongly against the NSDAP in elections.

(iv) However, the SPD and KPD rarely provided a united front against Hitler. Rivalry between the left wing parties meant that they were unable to form a permanent alliance against their common enemy.

Socialist/Communist Opposition to National Socialism after 1933

On taking power, Hitler took immediate action to crush his political opponents.

(i) The Reichstag Fire — 27th February 1933. Hitler blamed the fire on the Communists. This gave him an excuse to lock up leading members of the KPD and SPD.

(ii) *The Enabling Act 23rd March 1933* — Under this act all political parties except the NSDAP were eventually banned.

(iii) In May 1933, Hitler ordered attacks on SPD, KPD and Trade Union headquarters.

(iv) Hitler's secret police tracked down and arrested any person suspected of having Socialist or Communist sympathies. These people were often treated brutally.

Conclusion

It became extremely difficult for Hitler's political opponents to operate within Germany. Many fled from Germany and tried to continue their opposition to National Socialism by working abroad to expose the cruelty of the new regime.

Opposition to National Socialism by the Churches

Hitler was intolerant of any rival to his authority in Germany. However, he was wary of making attacks on the Church. The National Socialists did not attempt to crush the power of the Church in the brutal way they attacked their political rivals.

Reasons

(i) Many supporters of the NSDAP were Christians.

(ii) Violence against the churches could antagonise Christians outside Germany and provoke foreign opposition to National Socialism.

(iii) The established churches in Germany offered little organised resistance to National Socialism so there was no need for brutal repression.

Hitler's Attempts to Control the Power of the Church

(i) In July 1933, Hitler signed an agreement with the Roman Catholic Church — The Concordat. Hitler guaranteed the rights of Catholics in Germany. In return, the Pope promised that Catholics would not interfere in the running of the country.

(ii) In September 1933, Hitler appointed the National Socialist sympathiser Ludwig Mueller as Protestant Reichbishop. Hitler wanted all Protestants united under one Reich Church.

(iii) The National Reich Church was formed in 1936. This was an attempt to replace Christian beliefs and worship with National Socialist beliefs and worship of Hitler. In the National Reich Church, the swastika replaced the cross and the Bible was replaced by *Mein Kampf*. Only National Socialist sympathisers could preach.

Church Opposition to National Socialism

(i) At first, the Christian churches welcomed Hitler's seizure of power. Many churchmen had little sympathy with the Weimar Republic which, although it had allowed complete religious freedom, had tried to separate Church from State. Many Weimar leaders were openly atheistic and many devout Christians disapproved of the new atmosphere of permissiveness and sexual freedom which seemed to be a feature of the period.

(ii) In later years, some churchmen spoke out against the treatment of the Jews and other persecuted minorities. These churchmen received harsh treatment.

(iii) The established churches in Germany offered no organised resistance to Hitler. It was left to certain brave individuals, for example Pastor Niemoller, to speak out against the obvious breeches of Christian values which took place under Hitler's rule.

Summary

Although some brave churchmen did speak out against the brutality of the Nazis, generally the Church preferred to come to terms with the Nazi regime. Those who did protest were dealt with harshly.

PREPARATION FOR
KNOWLEDGE AND UNDERSTANDING
EXAMINATION QUESTIONS

You may be asked to give an account, explanation or show the importance of:

(a) An **event**, e.g., describe the Bolshevik takeover in October / November 1917.

(b) A **development**, e.g., explain why so many Scots emigrated abroad in the 19th century.

(c) An **action**, e.g., why were gas attacks seldom able to allow either side to gain a 'breakthrough' on the Western Front?

(d) An **attitude**, e.g., how important was the contribution of women to the war effort in changing attitudes towards women gaining the vote?

You should have a clear understanding of the **concepts** for each unit as they often form part of the question. The concepts are listed as follows:

Unit	Key Concepts
UNIT ONE Changing Life in Scotland and Britain	(i) Economy; (ii) Population; (iii) Technology; (iv) Industry; (v) Social Conditions; (vi) Employment; (vii) Government; (viii) Democracy.
UNIT TWO International Cooperation and Conflict	(i) Nation; (ii) Conflict; (iii) Cooperation; (iv) Peace; (v) Security.
UNIT THREE People and Power	(i) Government; (ii) Ideology; (iii) Power; (iv) Discontent; (v) Resistance; (vi) Revolution.

CREDIT PAPER — Knowledge and Understanding (Section A)

One question in the Credit Paper requires you to write a short essay of several paragraphs and it is important that you prepare for this type of question by working through the questions on pages 146–154.

- These 8-mark essay questions normally require you to make at least six points in order to gain full marks. However, if you make fewer points but develop them well you will also gain full marks.

- You should also note that you should not list points but write in paragraphs.

- If you are asked to show the importance of an event, attitude or development, make sure your answer includes a balanced judgement.

GENERAL PAPER — Knowledge and Understanding (Section A)

- Unlike at Credit Level, the questions will be based on a presented source.

- Use the information in the source to help you answer the question.

- Make sure you put the information in your **own words**.

- To gain full marks, you will have to include some **recalled knowledge** (information about the question but which is not in the source) in your answer.

EXAMINATION PREPARATION

Work your way through the questions for the contexts you are studying. Most of the questions are taken from past examination papers at either Credit or General Level.

UNIT 1 — Changing Life in Scotland and Britain, Context B: 1830–1930

UNIT 1 — Changing Life in Scotland and Britain
Context C: 1880s to present

Unit 2 — International Cooperation and Conflict
Context B: 1890s–1920s

Part One: 1890–1914

UNIT 3 — People and Power
Context C: Russia 1914–1941

Part Three: 1924–1941

UNIT 3 — People and Power
Context D: Germany 1918–1939

**The Effects on Germany of the end of the First World War and
the Peace Settlement**

The Formation and Characteristics of the Weimar Republic

PREPARATION FOR ENQUIRY EXAMINATION QUESTIONS

Enquiry skills questions ask you to **evaluate** a historical source and, in the case of Unit 1 — Changing Life in Scotland and Britain, use sources to select information and reach a conclusion on a given issue.

You may be asked to:	*Style of Question*
(i) Make an evaluation of the strengths and weaknesses of a source by looking at accuracy, authorship, purpose, contemporaneity, bias, exaggeration or consistency.	(i) *(a)* How **useful** is the source as evidence of . . .? *(b)* How **typical** is the evidence in the source about . . .?
(ii) Compare points of view expressed in two different sources.	(ii) How fully do sources . . . and . . . **agree** about . . .?
(iii) Identify and / or explain the points of view and / or actions described in the sources.	(iii) *(a)* What does the **author** of the source think about . . .? *(b)* Identify and explain the **attitude** of the author to . . .
(iv) Set a source in its wider historical context by mentioning the purpose, timing and significance of the content.	(iv) *(a)* What do you think were the **intentions** of the **author** . . .? *(b)* How fully do the sources **explain** what happened?
(v) Select and organise information from no more than three sources appropriate to a given issue.	(v) What evidence in the sources **supports** the view that . . .? What evidence in the sources **disagrees** with the view that . . .?
(vi) Draw a conclusion to a given issue by using both information in the sources and recalled knowledge.	(vi) Use evidence from the sources and your own knowledge to come to a **conclusion** on . . .

Some rules to remember in answering these types of question.

(i) A source is useful or valuable if:

    (a) The **author** (writer of the source) *lived at the time* and *experienced* or *witnessed* the events described.

    (b) The **content** of the source is *detailed* and is *accurate*.

    (c) The **language** of the source is not *exaggerated*.

(ii) Most sources must be treated with a degree of caution but especially the following ones:

(a) A **propaganda poster**, e.g., a World War One recruitment poster, is *biased* in that its *purpose* is to persuade people to join the army. To do that it will *exaggerate* the way things were.

Nonetheless, these sources are still useful. Such a source shows how the Government tried to persuade people to join the army at the time.

(b) A **painting** or **drawing**. The painter or artist (the author) might have set out to draw the event, action, building or person in a *biased* way. For example, a person could be drawn in such a way as to make the person look attractive or otherwise. A crowd scene might be made to look larger or smaller than it actually was, depending on what the artist was trying to show. A building of a mill might be made to look attractive or ugly, depending on the view of the artist. In other words, the artist can *exaggerate* features just like any other author.

Nonetheless, these sources, e.g., drawings of coal miners at work in 1842, present a visual impression at a time when there were very few photographs.

(c) **Cartoons** — They are always *exaggerated* to put over a point of view.

Nonetheless, cartoons which appeared in magazines like *Punch* also tried to put across a message to the readers. As a result, the cartoon is valuable in showing how the cartoonist felt about an issue.

(d) **Speeches** by people trying to defend their actions, e.g., Stalin defending collectivisation. These speeches tend to be very *one-sided* and miss out important pieces of information. They are often so *biased* that they are *not consistent* with other historical evidence.

Nonetheless, they show how people tried to defend their actions and often misled people in doing so.

TYPE (i) QUESTIONS

Make an evaluation of the strengths and weaknessess of a source by looking at accuracy, authorship, purpose, contemporaneity, bias, exaggeration or consistency.

Example — Unit Two — International Cooperation and Conflict, Context B: 1890s–1920s

Source A is taken from Adolf Hitler's book — *Mein Kampf*, published in 1925. Hitler fought on the Western Front during the First World War.

Source A

> Each one of the points of the Treaty of Versailles should be fixed in the minds and hearts of the German people until sixty million men and women find their souls aflame with the feeling of rage and shame. The common cry must be — "we will be armed again!"

Question: How useful is Source A as evidence of how Germans felt about the Treaty of Versailles?

Answer: Source A is useful because the **author** of the source was a German who had fought in the war. However, the **purpose** of the author, Adolf Hitler, in writing this source was to turn people against the Treaty and give their support to his party. The language used in saying "sixty million men and women find their souls aflame with the feeling of rage and shame" is **exaggerated**. Nonetheless, the overall view expressed is **consistent** with the disappointment and resentment many Germans felt at, for example, the loss of land to Poland, the level of reparations and the War Guilt Clause.

TYPE (ii) QUESTIONS

Compare points of view expressed in two different sources.

Example: — Unit Three — People and Power,
Context C: Russia 1914–1941

Sources B and **C** give evidence about the causes of discontent in Stalin's Russia.

In **Source B**, John Scott, a British engineer who worked in Russia in the 1930s, describes the situation in the town of Magnitogorsk.

As the Arctic winter broke suddenly into spring, Magnitogorsk changed beyond recognition. In early April, it was still bitter cold, everything was frozen solid. By May, the ground had thawed and the city was swimming in mud . . . welding became next to impossible as our ragged cables short-circuited at every step . . . Bubonic plague had broken out in three places not far from Magnitogorsk . . .

The resistance of the population was very low because of the undernourishment during the winter and consistent overwork. Sanitary conditions, particularly during the thaw, were appalling . . . By middle of May the heat was intolerable. In the barracks we were consumed by bed-bugs and other vermin, and at work we had trouble keeping to the job.

In **Source C**, Victor Serge.

The winter was frightful, despite the lessening of the famine towards the New Year. I went to hospital in Orenburg. It was run as efficiently as possible, but really all that it treated was poverty. It was filled with those whose sickness lay in undernourishment. Children were covered in cold sores; whole wards were full of peasants with bellies empty and worn-out clothes. Medical supplies were in such short supply that the same bandages were washed out and used over and over again. Nor shall I forget, in those miserable days, how we all heard a radio broadcast from a meeting of the workers of a collective farm. Passionate voices went on endlessly, thanking the 'leader' for the 'good life we lead' and twenty or so patients tortured by hunger, half of them collective farm workers themselves, listened to it all in silence.

Question: Do Sources B and C agree about the causes of discontent in Stalin's Russia? Give reasons for your answer.

Answer: Sources B and C are in **close agreement** about the causes of discontent in Stalin's Russia.

Source B states that in Magnitogorsk there was a shortage of food during the winter and that as a result of this, people were likely to suffer from illnesses such as the Bubonic plague.

Source C makes a **similar comment** about the shortage of food in Orenburg which led to the people having to enter hospital for treatment. At Orenburg, many of those who entered hospital were peasants who worked on the collective farms yet did not have enough food to survive.

However, Source C **in addition** mentions that a shortage of medical supplies existed and this must have added to the discontent. In addition, the Government's propaganda on the radio, stating the success of the collectivisation programme at a time when many were starving, also fuelled discontent.

Source B mentions the inadequate living conditions brought about by bad sanitary conditions, and barracks for houses in the new town of Magnitogorsk where vermin and bed-bugs flourished. These living conditions, **not mentioned** in Source C, were also a cause of discontent.

TYPE (iii) QUESTIONS

Identify and explain the points of view described in the sources.

Example: — Unit Three — People and Power,
Context D: Germany 1918–1939

Source D comes from a book written by Albert Speer, who joined the Nazi party in 1931 and became an important member of Hitler's government.

Source D

> There was hope and new ideas. The dangers of communism could be stopped and, instead of hopeless unemployment, Germany could move towards economic recovery. My mother saw an SA parade in the street. The sight of such discipline in a time of chaos, the impression of energy in a time of hopelessness, seems to have won her over.

Question: Discuss the attitude towards the Nazi party shown in Source D.

Answer: The author, Albert Speer, joined the party in 1931 and went on to become a leading Nazi so he obviously supports the rise of the Nazi party. He sees the Nazis as an answer to the threat of communism in Germany and believes that the Nazis can solve the problem of mass unemployment brought about by the depression. He describes the way in which people, including older people, were won over to the Nazis because they could bring order and discipline to Germany at a time of great chaos.

TYPE (iv) QUESTIONS

Set a source in its wider historical context.

Example: — Unit Two — International Cooperation and Conflict, Context B: 1890s–1920s

Source E was written by Sir Phillip Gibbs, who was a British representative at the Peace Conference.

Source E

> It was a peace of vengeance. It was very unfair. The economic terms of the treaty were mad. Germany had to pay for all the damage caused during the war. The impossibility of getting all this money from a defeated country was obvious even to the most ignorant schoolboy.

Question: How far do you agree with the author of Source E that Germany was unfairly treated at the Peace Conference? Use evidence from the source and your own knowledge to come to a conclusion.

Answer: I agree only to a **certain extent** with the author that Germany was unfairly treated at the Peace Conference. Given that Germany lost valuable land, rich in minerals, to Poland and the Saar coalfields to France, the means of repaying reparations was taken away from her.

However, I do not think that the terms were anywhere as vengeful as those Germany imposed on Russia and, in contrast, Germany lost very little land at Versailles.

I think that it was very unfair that Germany was not allowed to be represented at the conference and that she was held responsible for starting the war. There was no mention of reparations in Woodrow Wilson's Fourteen Points and I agree that the level of reparations was very high.

However, the loss of land was so little that I cannot agree that "it was a peace of vengeance".

TYPE (v) and (vi) QUESTIONS

Select and organise information appropriate to a given issue.

Draw a conclusion to a given issue by using both information in the sources and recalled knowledge.

Example One — Unit One — Context B: 1830s–1930s

The issue for investigating is:

Lack of hygiene was the main reason for the spread of disease in Scotland between 1830 and 1930.

Study the sources carefully and answer the questions which follow. You should use your own knowledge where appropriate.

Source F is from a report written in 1842 on the Sanitary Conditions of the Labouring Population of Scotland. This extract describes conditions in Stirling.

Source F

The filth of the prison floats down the public streets and gives off a disgusting smell. The slaughterhouse is near the top of the town, and the blood from it is allowed to flow down the public streets. There are no public toilets and the common stairs and closes, and even the public streets, are used as toilets.

Source G is an account by Dr Arnott of conditions in Glasgow in 1842.

Source G

In Glasgow, the great mass of the fever cases occurred in the areas in which the poorest lived. In these dwellings we saw half-dressed wretches crowding together to be warm. Although it was the middle of the day, several women were under a blanket, because other women were wearing the only set of clothes.
Who can wonder that disease should spread in such situations!

Source **H** is from a report about conditions in Greenock in 1842.

Source H

Most of the dwellings of the poor are in very narrow closes or alleys with little ventilation. The space between the houses is so narrow as to exclude the sun. The houses are generally two or three storeys high, divided into flats with four or five families in each flat. They have one or two rooms each of about eight to ten feet square.

Question: What evidence in the sources supports the view that lack of hygiene was the main reason for the spread of disease in Scotland between 1830 and 1880?

What evidence in the sources suggests that lack of hygiene was not the main reason for the spread of disease in Scotland between 1830 and 1880?

Answer: The evidence in Source F which supports the statement is that at a time of disease, waste from a prison was floating down the streets, blood from a slaughterhouse also flowed into the streets. The source also mentions people using closes and the streets as public toilets.

Source G mentions a number of people sharing the same bed and clothing.

The evidence in Source G which contradicts the statement is that poverty was also a cause of the spread of disease.

Source H mentions the narrow streets which allowed little ventilation, houses packed tightly together and many people being crammed into small rooms.

Question: How important do you think lack of hygiene was as a cause of the spread of disease in Scotland between 1830 and 1880? You should use evidence from the sources and your own knowledge to reach a balanced conclusion.

Answer: There is no doubt that lack of hygiene was an important cause of disease. **Typhus** spread as a result of poor personal hygiene and with overcrowded living conditions the disease spread quickly.

However, there were other reasons which were more significant in the spread of disease. The **absence of clean drinking water** resulted in the spread of both **cholera** and **typhoid**. As a result of sewage being deposited next to water supplies, there were serious epidemics of cholera and typhoid during this period. In addition, a **lack of medical knowledge** both about the cause of disease and an appropriate treatment did not help.

I think that the level of poverty was another major cause of disease with the young and elderly particularly vulnerable as a result of inadequate clothing, housing and food. Milk was not sterilized and this contributed to **tuberculosis**, the second greatest killer disease of the time.

In conclusion, I would say that the lack of clean drinking water, the absence of medical knowledge and overcrowded living conditions were the main causes of the spread of disease.

Example Two — Unit 1 — Context C: 1880s to Present Day.

The issue for investigating is:

> Housing in Scotland improved greatly between the 1880s and the 1930s.

Study the sources carefully and answer the questions which follow. You should use your own knowledge where appropriate.

In **Source I** Georgina Robertson describes girls' lodgings in Fraserburgh in 1891.

Source I

Many of the girls' rooms aren't fit for human habitation — smoky, dirty, draughty, without cupboards or shelves and only one bedstead to every three girls. The girls have to live, cook and wash, as well as sleep, in a very small space. But the most crying evil is the lack of toilets.

In **Source J** Nellie Edgar describes her new council house in Glasgow which she moved into in the 1930s.

Source J

My parents' room was the parlour too, so they had their bed in it and a three-piece suite. As well as that, we had a real living room separate from the kitchen, and a bathroom. No more tin tubs, and there was the garden.

In **Source K** Mollie Weir describes her childhood home in Glasgow in the 1930s.

Source K

We called our room and kitchen a house for we'd never heard of the word 'flat' when I was a wee girl. An outside toilet had to be shared with two other families. There were several large families living in a single room. One family had fourteen children and they all lived in one room.

Question: What evidence is there in the sources that housing in Scotland improved greatly between the 1880s and 1930s?

What evidence is there in the sources that housing in Scotland did not improve greatly between the 1880s and 1930s?

Answer: The evidence which supports the statement is that while Source I states that conditions in 1891 were very poor with overcrowded rooms and lack of decent toilets, source J shows some improvements by the 1930s with separate bedrooms and bathrooms.

The evidence in Source K which contradicts the statement is that people still appear to be living in overcrowded conditions with poor toilet facilities, i.e., sharing outside toilets.

Question: How greatly do you think that housing in Scotland improved between the 1880s and 1930s? You should use evidence from the sources and your own knowledge to reach a balanced conclusion.

Answer: Housing did improve during the period. In the 1880s, housing was very poor with severe overcrowding and poor sanitation, and this was particularly bad in cities like Glasgow and Edinburgh.

By the end of the 1930s, there were significant improvements. Council houses with indoor toilets, electricity and gardens were introduced after the war which the better-off working class could afford.

Most of the worst slums had been removed and very few people lived in one-roomed houses.

For the middle classes, a variety of styles of housing was introduced, from the grand Victorian / Edwardian mansions to the inter-war bungalows.

In the countryside, cottages were greatly improved and bothies were very rare by 1918.

In conclusion, it is clear housing improved greatly, although, for the very poor, inadequate slum housing continued to exist.

NOTES

NOTES

Printed by Bell & Bain Ltd., Glasgow, Scotland.